MANNY KHOSHBIN'S
Contrarian PlayBook

How to Build Your
$100 Million Real Estate Portfolio
From the Ground Up

MANNY KHOSHBIN'S
Contrarian PlayBook

How to Build Your
$100 Million Real Estate Portfolio
From the Ground Up

GeniusWork Publishing
Los Angeles

Published by GeniusWork Publishing
www.geniusworkpublishing.com

Printed in the United States of America
Cover Design: Sakura Reese
Cover Photograph: Damir K
Illustration: Sarah Lane

Publisher's Cataloging in Publication
    Khoshbin, Manny.
       Manny Khoshbin's contrarian playBook : how to build
    your $100 million real estate portfolio from the ground
    up.
      p. cm.
      Includes index.
      LCCN 2011938060
      ISBN-13: 978-0983139317
      ISBN-10: 0983139318

      1. Real estate investment.   I. Title.

HD1382.5.K46 2011   332.63'24
          QBI11-600187

This book is dedicated to my Mother and Father, with gratitude for the many sacrifices they made in order to bring our family to the United States.

Table of Contents

Introduction

I love real estate investment. I can't even imagine my life if I had not found my way to this work–although "work" is not the most accurate description of how I feel about it. For me, real estate investment is "play"–very serious play–but still play, in that I totally enjoy the process.

Riffing on another definition of play, I would say that there is a competitive thrill to real estate investment, and I don't mean the competition with other investors to buy a particular property. It is a competition you have with yourself, a commitment to always bring your best game to the table, because each real estate deal is unique, and therefore an adventure. And with this adventure comes real exhilaration.

So I invite you to jump into the game as a real estate investment "player." This book is intended to serve as a playbook, and contains the proven practices that make up my winning game plan: A solid strategy for extraordinary success in real estate investment. If followed, this book could start or spur the path that will take you to your $100 million real estate portfolio.

There are many things I love about real estate investment. I love the hunt of finding the right market, and the right property in that market. I love the negotiation involved in buying a property. I love working with a property once it is mine, and bringing it to its full potential. I love adding value to a property, and since there are many ways to do this, I get to be very creative. I love the pride of ownership I feel as a landlord. And when it is time, I love selling a property that I know I improved, and selling it at a significant profit.

While I love playing the game of real estate, I also enjoy the prosperity it brings. I am doing something I am passionate about and being richly rewarded by it. America is a land of opportunity, and real estate investment is a great way to make the most of all it has to offer.

I am excited to share this book with you and honored that you are here. In 1996, I found myself talking to my former landlord. He told me that I reminded him of himself as a young man when he first came to Orange County, California and started buying real estate. He suggested that I look at real estate investment as a possibility for my own career. He pointed out that if you take a handful of dirt and put it in your pocket today, you can hang your pants up and come back years later, and the dirt will still be there. As Mark Twain tells us, "Buy land, they've stopped making it."

In other words, real estate is a tangible asset, and as such is unique in the investment world. With these words, he planted the seed that I have now grown into my own success. In gratitude to him, I want to do the same for you–get you started, or reignited, in your own real estate investment career! I hope that you find yourself loving this game as much as I do.

I.

REAL ESTATE
IS THE WAY
TO GO

Let's Gooooo!

This book is not just about how to invest in real estate; it is about how to be a very successful real estate investor. In the pages to come, I will share my own powerful contrarian investing strategy, which is the foundation on which I built my $100 million (and growing!) real estate portfolio. I will also show you how to implement this strategy like a true contrarian, which will call on your commitment, common sense, and *cojones*!

You will see that no matter what your current situation, you can jump right in and start playing this game. In the playbook, you will find critical information and criteria to use at each stage of your portfolio development.

Finally, you will see how investing like a contrarian will allow you to create a full success, one where the investing itself feels as good as the financial rewards! After all, we all know that the best players play out of a love of the game.

From The Ground Up

When I say you can become a very successful real estate investor, I mean it! I can also say with complete confidence that it can work for you regardless of your starting point, because it got me where I am today—and I started out with absolutely nothing.

To this day, I drive by a supermarket parking lot that has a particular memory for me. As a young boy, my family lived in our car in that parking lot for months, surviving on nothing but bananas much of that time. My father had taken a bold step and moved our family of six from Iran to the United States, just weeks before my fourteenth birthday. We left behind a comfortable lifestyle—my father owned a hardware store and was a retired Senior Cost Accountant, and our home was completely paid off. My father made this risky move to protect me, because I was on the verge of being drafted into the Iranian army.

We were thrilled to come to the United States, but unfortunately, the job my father had been promised did not come through. We found ourselves with little money and nowhere to live. I still marvel at the fact that my father and mother never gave up. My father eventually found work, and we moved into a small apartment, but the experience of living in a car stays with you the rest of your life.

To help contribute some money to my family, I became a dumpster diver, selling the recovered items at swap meets on the weekends—my first business! Then, at the age of sixteen, I worked at Kmart, cleaning toilets and collecting shopping carts. This job served an important purpose, instilling in me the value of hard work and determination. It also taught me to remain focused on my long-term goals: I always knew that this job was only a stepping stone on a path to something much greater.

I had a strong entrepreneurial spirit, and was always interested in going into business for myself. While still in high school, I created my own multi-level marketing company. I later tried to open a Mobil gas station. At the age of twenty-one I got my real estate license and opened a mortgage company until the slowdown in 1994. At several points in this journey, I found myself back at square one—in other words, a failed business and zero money—but I never gave up, and never stopped planning my next move.

When my partner and I shut down our mortgage company in 1994, I suggested we try a 79 cents store, as competition to the 99 cents stores that were opening around us. The first store was a huge success, and when we expanded a second store to offer meat and produce, we celebrated the fact that our risk had paid off…until a Food4Less store moved in next door. For the next 18 months, we struggled. I worked seven days a week. I had to go to the bank twice a day: Before 10 a.m. to deposit funds to cover the overdraft charges from the night before, and again before 4 p.m. to deposit what we had sold to that point, with the hope that we could avoid the overdraft fees the next day. I was paying over $1,200 in non-sufficient fund fees per month.

The good news is that soon after, I found my way to real estate investment. I bought my first commercial property, a strip mall, in 1999. By 2002, I had brought my portfolio value to $1 million. Today the value of my real estate portfolio is well over $100 million. My real estate transactions total over $500 million: I have purchased over $300 million in real property, and sold over $200 million. I own over 1.5 million square feet of property in seven states, most notably in California and Texas. In addition, The Khoshbin Company, my commercial real estate management and investment firm, manages over 2.5 million square feet of real estate. The average return on my real estate deals has been thirty percent. I can proudly say that of the more than seventy buildings I have bought and sold, I have only sold two at a loss, both due to single tenants who vacated. The best part of all of this is that I am passionate about what I do, and the financial freedom I have achieved allows me to truly live life on my own terms.

Looking back, I see that it was indeed a blessing to start out with nothing. Not only did it teach me valuable lessons, it also gave me the ability to say, with total confidence, that I built my $100 million real estate portfolio—and the real estate investment strategy that I am about to share with you—from scratch.

This strategy has been shaped by my many mistakes as much as it has been by my successes. My journey to success in the

U.S.A has been an adventurous one, to say the least, and I've encountered my fair share of pitfalls along the way. It is with the intention of helping you to avoid making these same mistakes on the path to your own success that I share my strategy with you. No matter what your current circumstances, this book is designed to give you—step by step, and play by play—a powerful strategy for a wildly successful career in real estate.

Why You Will Love Real Estate Investment

Here is what some of the wealthiest Americans have said about real estate:

- "80 percent of all millionaires made it through real estate"
  – Andrew Carnegie
- "Real estate is the basis for all wealth."
  – Theodore Roosevelt

Real estate has been a lucrative investment for centuries, and over time outperforms most other types of investments. It is a tangible asset, and one that offers great leverage and tax advantages. Furthermore, real estate investment can bring high returns with reasonable risks.

As a tangible asset, real estate offers two unique benefits. One, you can take a pride of ownership in your real estate holdings. This pride of ownership is a hugely motivating factor for me, and one that I enjoy immensely. Two, as a tangible asset real estate has inherent value, and therefore more built-in security for the investor. Of course the value of your portfolio will fluctuate along with the economy, but if you choose your investments wisely you will have the assurance that, even in the event of a prolonged economic recession, the value of your real estate holdings will eventually rebound. As a general rule, you can count on real estate values going up over time due to supply/demand, population growth, and inflation of supplies and labor, which pushes up construction costs. Over the long run, these factors will also push up replacement values. History shows us that even in the rare cases where real estate values deflate for prolonged periods of time (such as the Great Depression), they eventually come back up–in a big way!

Real estate also offers the investor greater leverage at more favorable terms than other types of investments. For example, if you own stocks, you can leverage them by borrowing on margin–but if the value of the stock drops, you are at risk of a margin call. This is extremely risky, and many have lost their fortunes and entire portfolios during market corrections and crashes.

With real estate loans you do not carry such a risk. If your property drops in value, you simply maintain the property while you wait for the market to rebound–and with income property, you have the added bonus of collecting the lease revenue until the market is right to sell.

Also, with stocks you have little control over the management of your investment. This leaves you at the mercy of the company's leadership–and if the CEO is manipulating the stock options or the CFO is cooking the books (anybody recall Enron?), your investment could be what suffers. As a real estate investor, you enjoy a much higher level of control over the management of your assets.

Furthermore, tax laws benefit real estate investors. Making full use of the various tax benefits and considerations available to you will mean both an improved bottom line and a steady and sustainable growth of your real estate portfolio. In my case the tax system continually motivates me to expand my portfolio through options like depreciation and Section 1031 exchange, which we will look at more closely in a later section.

Last but not least, real estate investment is a dynamic path, and every deal is different, which keeps things interesting! I love the wealth it has brought me, but I am also grateful for the joy I get from playing the game. It is my love for the game that makes me excited to get up and get to work each day.

Real estate, like any other type of investment, is not without risk—but in my experience, if you take calculated risks, you will find that they are more than offset by the rewards. Of course, I have been able to enjoy these benefits because I have the foundation of a solid investment strategy. If you study and implement the game plan laid out for you in this book, I am confident that not only will you love real estate investment, but it will love you back!

II.
THE GAME

The Goal
Your $100 Million Real Estate Portfolio

$100 million is a good goal, especially if it is banked in your real estate portfolio. As a good goal, it should motivate and inspire you. A good goal also makes the game more interesting! It keeps you on course and allows you to focus your attention and energy more precisely, which will make you a better player. So say "YES" to your $100 million real estate portfolio!

Take note that your goal will continue to grow alongside your wealth. As a kid, my goal was to make enough money to buy my parents and myself a house, and to drive a nice car. Once I achieved that, I set my sights on $1 million–and once I met that goal, I set my sights on $100 million. It took me some time to reach the $100 million milestone, but once I did, I raised the bar even higher for myself: I am now aiming for $1 billion! The way I see it, it may take me 5, 10, or 15 years to get there– but this is time that would be passing anyway! I might as well spend it achieving my dreams.

If it is difficult to clearly envision $100 million, think of it in terms of the tangible assets you will own. How many office buildings do you see as your goal? You can also envision the lifestyle that is at the heart of your goal. Imagine your financial freedom: The freedom to choose where you live, the size of your home, the car (or cars!) that you drive, the places you travel to, the charitable causes you support, and–most importantly– how you spend your time, without money being the deciding factor. Personally, I feel truly blessed to have an abundance of resources to share with my family and friends. This motivates and inspires me every day.

This being said, the greatest marker of my success–beyond the value of my portfolio–is the fact that I love what I do. I am fortunate enough to truly love my work as a real estate investor. Loving your work makes the path to success an enjoyable one, and helps you to rise above the challenges you encounter along the way. It is a powerful feeling to realize that you really can make your own destiny!

The Winning Mindset
Think Like a Contrarian

---

con ·trar i ·an

[kuhn-trair-ee-uhn]

—noun

a person who takes an opposing view, esp. one who rejects
the majority opinion, as in economic matters.

Being a contrarian is at the core of my success as a real estate investor. As a contrarian I do not run with or after the pack, but rather use my powers of common sense to blaze my own trail. In this way, I am able to stay ahead of the curve, and prosper greatly in the process. Common sense really is king! The contrarian way keeps me grounded in sound investing principals, while others around me give in to fear or greed.

While we all know it is very sensible to buy low and sell high, it is also much easier said than done, and the investors who follow this sound advice–the true contrarians–are few and far between. As it turns out, buying low and selling high requires the ability to overcome the influence of your emotions. Of course, nobody ever wants to lose money, but more often than not, both greed and fear lead people to miss out on good opportunities to buy and sell at a profit.

For example, I have seen even experienced investors lose their shirts by getting greedy at the top of the market. They turn down opportunities to sell high because they think that if they wait just a little longer, they might be able to sell even higher! All too often, the market turns and the opportunity is gone. Contrarians, on the other hand, will seize the opportunity to sell high and later reinvest the profits into lower risk distressed property, thereby expanding their portfolios, growing their wealth, and getting that much farther ahead of the pack. Meanwhile, the investors who got greedy are sitting on their hands, waiting for the market to come back up.

Other investors let their fear of paying too high a price paralyze them. Instead of jumping in and buying at a good price, their fear worries them out of deals that would make them money. You can see how greed and fear overlap, and in the end can ruin the best opportunities. It is human nature to let these emotions shape your decisions, but in real estate investment this is a mistake that will cost you big, every time.

Interestingly, another emotion to be aware of is love. As much as I love the game of real estate investing, I do not allow myself to get attached to my properties. It is too easy to "fall in love" with a property and get so emotionally vested in it that you do not make wise investment decisions. I would be willing to sell even the house I own now, which I am very happy in, for a good profit. If you are looking to buy your dream house, that is fine—but understand that it is not the same as real estate investment.

The contrarian has the common sense to steer clear of these pitfalls and the cojones to make bold moves, no matter what direction the pack is heading. The contrarian is not reckless, but is willing to do the work and commit to full-on action!

Of all the skills that will enable you to successfully play the game of real estate investment, thinking like a contrarian tops the list. It is a winning mindset!

The Game Plan
Make Your Money on the Buy

As I mentioned before, one of the things I love most about real estate investment is that it is a very dynamic process, with many moving parts. This book will give you a clear view of the big picture of real estate investment, and specific steps (plays) to take, regardless of your current circumstances or level of experience. If you are a new investor, there is valuable information that will get you started and ready for the more advanced investment strategy. If you are already a part-time investor, this is the strategy that could take you full-time. If you are a seasoned investor, you will find that this book will up your game on all levels.

My game plan is simple but solid: Make your money on the buy! It revolves around the classic contrarian principle of buy low, sell high. Instead of buying flashy new buildings, I invest exclusively in discounted properties—the diamonds in the rough. I find a property that is discounted, then with a smart initial offer and full attention to the due diligence period, I am able to negotiate further discounts, increasing the money I make on the buy. I then take an active role in my portfolio and property management, and because I purchased underperforming properties, I can easily add value to them. Once I have increased the value of the properties, I continue to make money by leasing, then—when the time is right—selling high.

Finally, I am always expanding my horizons; I currently have investments in seven states. Instead of waiting for my local market to shift, I go to the markets that are ready for me.

Don't Speculate

It is important to note the difference between the Contrarian PlayBook strategy and speculative investing. The desire to have your name attached to a flashy new property is understandable, and is common amongst real estate investors. Not coincidentally, it is also one of the biggest obstacles to successful real estate investment.

Buying new construction is pure speculation, and investors who go this route are risking everything with what is, essentially, a bet on the direction of the market. In 2004, my buddies bought into the flashy new property of the month—the MGM condos in Vegas—and told me I was crazy not to: "It's only $500k, you're on the 30th floor, with beautiful views, and MGM will rent it for you!" It didn't make sense to me. I sensed the hype, and told them I'd rather buy a nice income property instead. I knew that while real estate investment of any kind bears some degree of risk, I would be taking a much more calculated risk by buying an older property with existing tenants. I was right in the end—my buddies lost a lot of money.

At one point, Nevada had 110 high-rise developments in their planning department. After the recession started in 2007, 60-70 were canceled. The same thing happened in Dubai and Florida. Investors all follow each other, like a herd of sheep. Nobody wants to miss out on the next big thing. Meanwhile, contrarians stay away from speculative investing, and, in the end, win big!

Speculative investing is a gamble, not wise investing, and has no place in the Contrarian PlayBook strategy. Why gamble when you can use your common sense and make money in the process?

The Playbook

The playbook contains twelve plays, which are divided into three sections: Power Up, Make Your Money on the Buy, and Stay in the Game. Each of these sections represents a distinct phase of the Contrarian PlayBook strategy. I have no doubt that if you follow this strategy and stick with it, it will take you all the way to your $100 million real estate portfolio–from the ground up!

Overview of the Plays:

Power Up

Play #1. Set Your Goals

Set specific long and short-term financial goals, making sure that your short-term goals will lead you to your long-term goals. Assess your current financial situation–as well as your risk tolerance–as both are key factors in how you will build your $100 million portfolio.

Play #2. Get Smart, Get Credible

Knowledge is power, so power up! Analyze the economy and real estate markets, so that you can invest in the right place, at the right time and stay ahead of the curve. Become a real estate agent so you can take your game to new levels! Last but not least, get credible: Establishing your personal and financial credibility will pave the way for every deal you ever make.

Play #3. Use Your Resources

Maximize the resources available to you! Build your "team" of bankers, real estate experts, and other industry professionals who will help you on the path to your $100 million real estate portfolio. Know your financing options, and find out what financing you qualify for! Learn about the various tax benefits and considerations available to real estate investors.

Make Your Money on the Buy

Play #4. Select Your Property Type: Residential

Learn the pros and cons of the various residential property types, and determine which one is the best fit for you at each stage of your portfolio development.

Play #5. Pick a Winner: Residential

Use the critical criteria to help you identify the residential properties that will be your best investments.

Play #6. Select Your Property Type: Commercial

Learn the pros and cons of the various commercial property types, and determine which one is the best fit for you at each stage of your portfolio development.

Play #7. Pick a Winner: Commercial

Use the critical criteria to identify the commercial properties that will be your best investments.

Play #8. Negotiate From Strength

Once you've found the right property, you will need to hone your negotiation skills! Use your credibility to your fullest advantage. "Give to Get" in your negotiations, and get the deal done! Successfully navigate every stage of the negotiation process, from the first contact with the seller's agent to the initial offer, from due diligence to the final inspection. Make your money on the buy!

Stay in the Game

Play #9. Add Value to Your Properties

Understand the value of potential. Now that you've made your money on the buy, raise the value of your properties by making cosmetic improvements, leasing up, and trimming operating expenses!

Play #10. Actively Manage Your Properties

Take a hands-on approach with your properties, and an engaged role with your tenants, by maintaining a consistent onsite presence. "Give to Get" with your tenants, and treat them like your partners—because that's what they are!

Play #11. Actively Manage Your Portfolio

Learn the fundamentals of portfolio management. Understand the important role of liquidity, and make your properties work for you. Buy and sell on contrarian time, and hold like an active investor!

Play #12. Expand Your Horizons

Stay on top of the game by staying ahead of the curve! Identify the right time to branch out into new territories—after all, in the

U.S.A. you have 50 unique economies, and (thanks to the internet) all the information you need is right at your fingertips!

As you can see, the plays make good common sense–contrarian sense! Following them will allow you to buy low, lease up, then sell high. By starting the process with a strong, discounted buy, you will be on much more solid ground as you move forward. This is why making your money on the buy is so pivotal to the Contrarian PlayBook strategy.

To summarize:
- In order to buy low:
  - Buy discounted properties, including underperforming and/or distressed properties
  - Negotiate further discounts with your offer, during the due diligence period, and upon final inspection
- In order to sell high:
  - Add value to your properties
  - Actively manage your properties
- To truly skyrocket your portfolio's value:
  - Actively manage your portfolio
  - Expand your portfolio into new territories

Dream it. Do it. Live it.

I decided to write this book because I realized that I wanted to help others to achieve their dreams, just as I have. So while I am proud to be giving you a solid and well-rounded real estate investment strategy, I wouldn't be giving you a complete picture of this strategy without also sharing some of the experiences that have made me who I am today. These experiences have played a major role in shaping both my approach to life and my approach to real estate investment, which in many ways are one and the same. Knowing the rules is only part of the game—tuning into your drive, passion and individual strengths is what will make you a great player. With this in mind, the playbook also contains a few narrative snapshots of my journey to success. I hope you find them motivating and inspiring.

III.
THE PLAYBOOK

POWER UP

DREAM IT!

One of the keys to success is the ability to dream, and to dream big–that's where it all starts! A dream that inspires you to get up and get to work each day will power you through all the ups and downs you encounter along the way. In the game of achieving remarkable success as a real estate investor, keeping your eye on the prize means staying in touch with your dreams.

This has certainly been true for me. I was just a teenager when my family of six arrived in the U.S. The challenges we faced were daunting: Our first few months were spent living in our 1972 station wagon, and when we finally moved into our first apartment in this country, we were still faced with the many challenges of poverty. From the get-go, I dreamed of one day achieving true financial freedom for myself and my family. This dream is what initially fueled my current success.

I started with the desire to do anything I could to help my family. Remember, they all left Iran to protect me from being drafted into the Iranian army, an army where young men were used to find the landmines because, in the government's view of things, the young draftees were more expendable than tanks. To this day, many of my uncles who were drafted have not fully recovered from their injuries. Sadly, one of my uncles recently passed at age fifty-two, after a twenty-year battle with cancer caused by chemical bombs from the war.

My commitment to help contribute to my family was strong, but since I was underage and did not speak English well, I had to be inventive about my first business endeavor. I became a dumpster diver, and a good one at that! I figured out the routes of all the garbage trucks in our neighborhood and was able to hit each dumpster at just the right time. I quickly had a thriving business selling at the weekend swap meet, and within months needed two spaces to hold all of my "finds."

Every job I took from that point on, from cleaning toilets and pushing shopping carts at Kmart to going door-to-door selling packaged fruits and nuts, was fueled by my dream of financial stability for myself and my family.

These early jobs taught me a great deal about hard work and persistence, but they were difficult in more ways than one. Like many immigrants, an obstacle that I had to face early on was prejudice. When I first started my job at Kmart, I avoided the cafeteria where the other employees called me "camel rider"– but because I had a dream, I was able to turn every insult into a positive incentive. I told myself, "It's ok. Let them say what they want to say. I will succeed no matter what!" Within months, I was promoted to a management position, and I was named Employee of the Month four times in the sixteen months I worked there. Dreams are powerful allies, no matter what the world throws at you!

My dream of financial success also saw me through some tough times as a young entrepreneur. During the year and a half that I worked as an assistant manager at a tire store, I had to get up at 4 a.m. and drive an hour to work, six days a week, but I did it–fueled by my dream of a life beyond that job. The dream also provided the incentive for me to save $25,000 in my time there. Everything was going according to plan, until a business broker exhausted all of my savings and left me high and dry, instead of helping me open a Mobil gas station as he said he would. After years of working and saving, I was back to square one.

It would have been very easy to give up at that point. I could have convinced myself that I would never be successful at business. But when you have a dream, you don't give up. When you have a dream, you know that overcoming obstacles is just part of the game. When you have a dream, you keep your goal in clear sight, pick yourself up, and get going again!

Today, the dream I started with has continued to grow with my success. My dream is still my north star. Find a dream that truly inspires you, and you will find a way to make it a reality. Remember that no dream is too big—your only limitation is your imagination.

Let's Gooooo!

Play #1

Set Your Goals

Set Your Long-Term Goal: Name Your Number

Everyone has a number—the minimum amount of money you believe will give you the financial freedom you want to have in your life. This could mean $5 thousand, $5 million, or $5 billion. Practically speaking, this number could mean paying off your car, retiring from your job, buying a beachfront property, or traveling the world—and it is important to remember that this number is as much about your happiness as it is about the money itself.

I find it hard to believe when someone says they don't care about money. In our society, money is always a factor. Money may be just a dirty piece of paper, but if you make it work for you, it is an incredibly powerful tool. As a tool, money can give you security, time, and the freedom to choose your lifestyle–in other words, financial freedom! What you do with this freedom is entirely up to you. Ultimately, my goal in sharing my real estate investment strategy with you is to help you arrive at your own financial freedom, and to give you the knowledge you will need to make wise choices along the way.

As you know from the subtitle of this book, I am naming the $100 million real estate portfolio as a good value to set as your bar. If this number doesn't do it for you, pick one that does! By creating a target that gives you both focus and incentive, you dramatically increase your chances of success. Find the number that inspires you to jump into the game. Nothing is impossible–don't be intimidated by setting very large goals! In this case, a number is worth a thousand words.

Set Your Short-Term Goals

If the function of a good long-term goal is to inspire, the purpose of a good short-term goal is to translate inspiration into action! Many people set a long-term goal, then have no idea how to begin. In order to achieve your bigger goals, you will need to take a series of smaller steps in the right direction. To travel from California to New York by car, you can only see the road in front of you. You can't see the Statue of Liberty at the beginning of your trip, so as much as the idea of being in New York might inspire you, you will never get there unless your plan includes the short-term goal of driving out of California!

Some short-term goals may require you to make changes in your life. If you are unable to save money for a down payment on a property in your current job, get a second job. If you don't qualify for a mortgage loan, you may have to get a job that will qualify you. You might also consider taking that Hawaiian vacation money and using it as a down payment on a condo instead.

Don't be afraid to change your short-term goals if they are not working! Before I turned my focus to real estate investing, I had, among others, retail and mortgage businesses. I dedicated myself fully to these endeavors, but none of them were getting me to my long-term goal of financial freedom, so I made a change. No matter what your current circumstances, the most important thing is to take action now, and to take action in a way that supports your long-term goal.

Your short-term goals can include specific financial targets as well as specific actions. In the first year, for instance, you might target adding two new income properties and $100,000 of value to your real estate portfolio. Remember that while these initial goals may seem a long ways from your long-term goal, once you get the ball rolling, your real estate portfolio can expand exponentially. Be patient, and keep your eye on the prize.

Finally, be sure to set short-term goals that are within reach. One of the most common mistakes I see new investors make is setting unrealistic goals for themselves, and then getting discouraged and giving up when they are unable to meet them. Flexibility is important, and if you are not flexible enough to adapt to changing circumstances, you will not be able to make full use of the strategy laid out for you in this book.

Assess Your Current Financial Situation

In order to set realistic short-term goals, you will need to take stock of your finances. An honest and realistic assessment is an important step—don't turn away from this task!

If you are debt-free and have money in the bank, great! Keep in mind that you do not need a huge amount in your savings account to get started. Many people think that real estate investment is out of their league unless they have $50,000 in the bank—but that's not true. Remember, my strategy is all about building your portfolio from the ground up.

In 1999, I advised a friend to buy a condominium for $65,000. She qualified for an FHA loan and only put $1,200 down. A year later, she sold it for $105,000 and bought a 4-plex apartment building. She then transitioned into a 6-unit apartment building, and finally into a 12-unit complex. By 2005, she had made $770,000 on her initial investment. From $1,200 to $770,000—she took a small savings and turned it into a lot of money!

If you do have debt, look it squarely in the eyes and then do what it takes to eliminate that debt by increasing your income and/or stepping up your savings strategy. As I said before, this may mean getting a second job, and/or making big changes to your lifestyle. It may mean giving up that Hawaiian vacation now, but just think of the vacations you will take once your $100 million portfolio is in place!

In the short term, simply thinking in terms of getting out of debt may make you feel quite far away from your long-term goals, and it may feel like great sacrifices are required—but trust me, it will be well worth it in the end!

As a teenager, one of my short-term goals was to get a car. I was working for $3.25 an hour at Kmart, and I saved the $4,000 I needed in just one year! We were paid weekly, and each week I would save almost all of the money. For example, if I was paid $121, I would take out $21 and seal the rest in an envelope, which I literally put under my mattress. Instead of buying my lunch at the cafeteria, I would bring sandwiches from home. I also saved money by not buying any brand name products. I made lots of small sacrifices every day, but the reward was great: A 1983 Burgundy Honda Accord!

Learning to save early on was a blessing, and a practice I carried into my adult life. As I told you, I saved $25,000 in a year and a half working as an assistant manager at a tire store. On the salary I was receiving, saving this much money required a conscious effort. I made this effort because I had a goal, and I knew that my sacrifices would pay off in the end.

Assess your Risk Tolerance

Just as it is important to set realistic short-term goals, it is also important to set short-term goals that won't overextend you, financially or personally. A good short-term goal can be reached with hard work, but without sleepless nights. I am a great advocate for action, and the right action should always be balanced with good judgment.

Understanding your risk tolerance will help you arrive at this balance. Every person's risk tolerance is different, and it is incredibly important to accurately assess and operate within yours. There is always risk in investing, but you should not shy away from looking at the worst-case scenario and asking yourself if you could handle it.

There is also an age factor to risk tolerance. Are you 30-40 years out from retirement, or are you 10-20 years out? Are you single, or are you married with children? If the market enters a down cycle, do you have the patience and resources to wait it out? It is important to answer these questions honestly.

If the steps you are taking to reach your long-term goal are causing you to lose sleep at night, then they are outside of your risk tolerance. For instance, you might take money out of your personal residence to buy an income property, which then leaves your home more exposed. If this sounds too scary to you, don't do it. There are always other alternatives. For instance, you could take a second job, or use some of your 401K. Risk tolerance is a highly subjective issue, and only you can determine yours.

Final Thoughts

The purpose of the Contrarian PlayBook is to give you a powerful, strategic approach to the game of successful real estate investment. This approach is based on my many years of experience, and shaped by both my successes and failures. There is a very good reason why Play #1 is about setting your goals: Your long-term goals give you destinations, and your short-term goals keep you focused along the way.

Remember, at the end of the day the real objective behind your financial goals is the financial freedom that money can provide. Whether you want to make a lot of money so you can spend it, save it, or give it all away, the freedom to choose how you spend your time and resources is the ultimate definition of success, and setting goals that really motivate you is the first step to achieving this success. Go ahead—dive in!

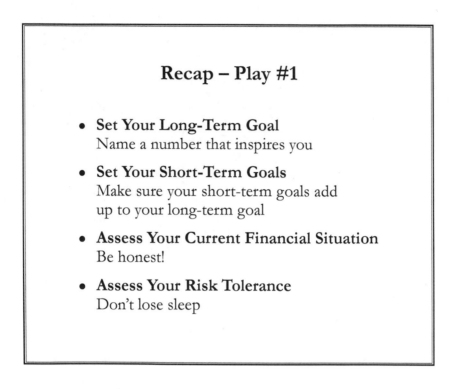

Recap – Play #1

- **Set Your Long-Term Goal**
  Name a number that inspires you

- **Set Your Short-Term Goals**
  Make sure your short-term goals add
  up to your long-term goal

- **Assess Your Current Financial Situation**
  Be honest!

- **Assess Your Risk Tolerance**
  Don't lose sleep

Play #2

Get Smart, Get Credible

Knowledge is Power

One of the keys to being a successful real estate investor is being an active investor, and a big part of being an active investor is educating yourself on an ongoing basis. You can never learn too much, and things are changing all the time, in the economy at large and in the real estate market specifically. Furthermore, the more knowledgeable you are, the more credible you will appear to other real estate professionals. It will also keep you ahead of the curve, and staying ahead of the curve is the hallmark of the contrarian investor. Knowledge is power, so power up!

Stay Ahead of the Curve

Staying ahead of the curve is all about timing. My friend calls me the Indiana Jones of real estate investing, because I understand the immense value of making bold decisions at the right time—bold, but never reckless. The reason I am able to make bold moves and win big, time after time, is that I know how to read the cycles of the real estate markets, and I am constantly gathering and analyzing a variety of information from a variety of sources.

Doing my own research allows me to spring into action on my own time, instead of waiting for the pundits to tell me it is time to buy, or time to sell—because by the time they announce it to the masses, it is too late! When they are telling you to buy, everyone will be buying, and all the best deals will be gone. When everyone is selling, it is more difficult to sell at a profit. Most people follow the trends, but you want to break away and put yourself in front of the pack. This is, after all, what being a contrarian is all about: Thinking on your feet, and staying ahead of the curve. It is also about having the cojones to make your decisions before they are validated by the crowd. Finally, it is about taking action, even if everyone around you thinks you are crazy!

With this in mind, your first step in breaking away from the pack is to do your own research about what's going on in the economy on a national, state, and local level. There are countless sources that you can utilize for your ongoing research. For general economic and real estate market news, I regularly read Moody's, CNBC, the Wall Street Journal, and Costar and Loopnet Reports, all available online. Focus your news gathering to four or five websites that you trust, and get in the habit of checking the sites regularly. Staying current will inform your instincts and keep them on track.

Analyze the Economy and the Real Estate Market

Common sense will tell you why being attuned to economic fluctuations is essential to anyone who wants to become (or remain) wealthy, from real estate or any other investment vehicle. One way or another, your success depends on what is happening in the economy—and the degree to which you do your research and are able to interpret your findings will be a deciding factor in your success.

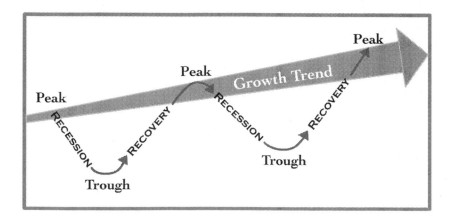

Economic Cycles

As the chart above shows, the economy is always in motion—but if nothing else, you can count on the fact that what goes up, must come down, and what goes down, must come up! History bears this out, time and again. Understanding this is one thing—knowing how to successfully time your investing to these cycles is another, and is the primary focus of this play.

Whether you are looking at the economy on a national, state, or local level, there are many variables—some predictable, others not—that play a role in shaping market conditions. All of these variables can create additional peaks and valleys in the very neat graphic above. For this reason, analyzing the direction of a specific economy or real estate market is always as much art as science, even with the wealth of statistics and data available to us nowadays. In reality, every cycle is at least slightly different, both in duration and in shape.

That said, economic cycles typically run around 60 months from peak to peak. This puts the trough at around the 30-month marker. A basic understanding of this cycle will help you to contextualize the data you uncover while researching state and local economies.

It is important to note that every state and local economy is going to have its own cycles to analyze. When it comes to real estate, this is significant because if it's a bad time to buy in one place, it could be a great time to buy somewhere else. This is true when comparing states, cities, or even neighborhoods! Doing your research will help you to determine if a specific state, city or neighborhood economy is in recovery or recession, and if it is close to a peak point, or a trough point. Since you want to buy in recessions before the recovery starts and sell through the recovery and peak, your research findings will indicate whether you should be buying, selling, or holding your properties in a given location.

The research process described in this play will be used throughout your portfolio development, and serves the same purpose whether you are looking at a broad market (i.e. a state or regional area) or a specific submarket (i.e. a neighborhood or commercial area).

State & Local Considerations

In order to keep you ahead of the curve, your research process needs to include keeping tabs on the various forces that drive the economy of a market or submarket. For instance, it was the rising oil prices and population growth in Texas in 2004 that alerted me to investment opportunities in the state. Their commercial real estate market was in a trough, which was indicated by the fact that there were many quality office buildings for sale at discounted prices. I was aware that Texas' economy was largely dependent on the state of the oil industry, so I knew that the economy would rebound with the price of oil—and that real estate values would follow suit. Turns out I was right—and when the economy and real estate markets made their comeback, I made a lot of money there as a result!

It is important to note that the initial slump in Texas' economy was at odds with the national economy as a whole, as well as the state economy of California (where I live), which was nearing the peak point in its cycle at the time. I might have assumed that Texas' cycle was mirroring California's—and if I had, I would have missed out on the buying opportunity of a lifetime! Likewise, if I hadn't done my research and learned that oil prices were coming back up, I wouldn't have gotten the notion that Texas would be a good place to invest. Being up-to-date is what kept me ahead of the curve, enabling me to clearly see the opportunities in the great state of Texas well before the rest of the pack caught on. This is the contrarian's vantage point!

Note: The story above is a great example of how the economies of different markets can vary, and how important it is to do your own research on these economies. That said, I want to point out that investing out-of-state is an advanced strategy, and not recommended for beginning investors. If you are a newer investor, keep in mind that you will want to apply these research techniques closer to home.

As I said before, the research you do serves the same purpose on the city and neighborhood (submarket) level as it does on the state level, but will be somewhat more focused. In order to get a preliminary feel for a city or neighborhood, I look at a variety of statistical data, such as population growth or decline. This is a big one—I rarely buy properties in cities where the population is going down, because a declining population can indicate a declining regional economy; after all, people go where the jobs are. Also, a declining population means less demand, and if there isn't enough demand in the submarket, you may have trouble selling down the line.

Other news to look at:

- Unemployment
- The economic health of major local industries
- Quality of life issues for the community
    - Including community development and services
- Local residential and commercial development

Generally, at this level of research you are casting a broad net, looking for something that sparks your interest because it could also spark a turn in the submarket's economy. If you come across information that piques your interest, it is probably worth analyzing further. More in-depth research is critical at this point, because, for instance, a significant low could either be an indicator that it is a great time to buy or a warning to stay away from that city or neighborhood. In order to make that distinction, you need to go deeper with your research.

Go Deeper

The focus of this phase of your research will be on analyzing specific real estate market data for the submarket(s) you are interested in. For residential properties you can search the term "housing market reports," and you will see over 200,000,000 hits! Personally, I use Zillow (www.zillow.com) for residential properties. Among other reasons, Zillow is great because you can easily see 10-year history charts for the residential property market in a given area.

Looking at historical housing market data, especially when charted, can tell you a lot. Unfortunately, it can't tell you with complete certainty where things are going, but it can indicate the trend, upward or downward. By studying the historical peaks and troughs, and comparing them to current information, you can see how much likely room there is to play with. Again, there are many variables that factor in, so there are no guarantees about where an economy or real estate market is going to go–but the more effective your research, the better your predictions.

Some of the reports I look at include:

- Home Value Index
- List Price
- Sale Price
- List Price Per Square Foot*
- Sale Price Per Square Foot*
- Listings With Price Cuts
- Amounts of Price Cuts
- Decreasing Values (%)

*The price per square foot is my favorite statistic to work with. It is simple but very revealing. I like to call it the "price per pound."

You will find these reports, and more, on the Zillow site, under "Local Info." By looking more closely at this data, you will get a more accurate picture of the area where you are considering investing. If the data suggests that the area is in a recession—property values have dropped, property sales are down, the number of listings with price reductions has increased—then it is a good time to buy low. You should, however, first check the data to be sure that the market is showing signs of stabilization. Use what you know about the various forces driving that submarket's economy to gauge the likelihood of an upcoming upturn—if the prospects look good, you might very well be ahead of the curve on this, and be able to buy before everyone else starts to catch on.

The internet provides a variety of places to find real estate market data. I recommend that you focus on one site for residential property information, and one site for commercial properties. For commercial properties, which are the only properties I buy beyond a 40-50 mile radius of my home and business, I use a Premier membership at Loopnet. It gives you historical sales, lease, and occupancy rates for all submarkets. Some investors also use Costar (www.costar.com). Regardless of which site you use, the process of determining where the economic cycle of a particular market or submarket is headed remains the same.

Note: I regularly pull historical sales figures on specific complexes or neighborhoods from the MLS sites, but keep in mind that to really get to much of the important data on these sites you will need to work with an experienced realtor, or be a licensed real estate agent yourself.

Final Research

There are two other pieces to analyzing a submarket's economic situation that should be included in your game plan, and both are essential. First, talk to local bankers, real estate agents, or anyone else who has an ear to the ground about what is happening in a particular market or submarket. When talking to real estate agents, introduce yourself as an interested buyer/investor and ask to be referred to the top broker at the firm. Take that person to lunch—get the inside scoop on the local economy, potential deals, and what's in the pipeline in general. They will know things that you won't be able to find online!

Finally, check out the submarket in person. Online research is important, but there is no substitute for feet on the ground. When you are at the point of focusing on a very specific submarket, you might take a simple walk around the neighborhood, meeting the dog walkers and joggers, or a drive around a commercial area to check out freeway accessibility. You will uncover valuable information from these in-person visits.

Case in point: I was considering a multi-unit apartment building in Long Beach, CA. On paper, this property looked very promising. Unfortunately, when I visited the property, I noticed it was across from a park that was populated by many homeless people, which negatively affects the property value. This is the type of information you can only find by physically touring the site.

In another instance, I was looking at a home in Santa Ana, CA. When I visited the property, I found that it was across from a huge apartment complex. Due to the higher traffic and tenant turnover of large apartment buildings, nearby residences are often at increased risk of vandalism.

In both cases, I was glad that I took the time to visit the properties myself. To this day, I never invest in a new market without personally scouting out the area first.

Your Next Move

As a contrarian you buy low and sell high, so you know that it is not a good idea to buy at the peak of the market. While it is possible to find deals on discounted and distressed properties during any market cycle, in a seller's market they are much fewer in number. There will also be more competition from other buyers, and therefore less leverage for you during negotiations with the seller. Never chase a property in a bidding war!

If you are a new investor and are therefore only looking at properties in your local area, your best strategy during a peak in the market would be patience. This doesn't mean that you should just sit on your hands in a seller's market. Use the downtime to further educate yourself on real estate investment so that when the market turns, you will be poised to make the most of it. If you are a more advanced investor, you might look at the housing markets in other states: There is more on this part of the game plan in Play #12.

The focus in this section has been on looking at both state and local economic factors to determine whether or not it is a good time to buy in a given location. In later plays, you will be given information on how to identify and locate the right properties within a given market.

Overall, when it comes to analyzing the economy and real estate markets I always keep the big picture in mind, use my common sense, and—because I have been doing this long enough—listen to my instincts. I don't get caught up in trying to buy at the absolute bottom, because experience has taught me that it is impossible to time the market exactly. It is not about perfection, it is about adding value to your portfolio by negotiating that great deal and making your money on the buy!

Become a Real Estate Agent

I could beat around the bush with this, but I'm just going to say it: Get your real estate license! In terms of becoming knowledgeable about real estate, I guarantee it will be the best time and money you could spend. The skill and knowledge that you will acquire will benefit you each and every step of the way, from finding the best investments to securing the best deals. You will learn about lending regulations, how properties are valued and appraised, and so much more. Getting your real estate license will make you a wiser investor, even if you never sell anything to an outside party. It will also give you unrestricted access to the Multiple-Listing Service (MLS) sites you will be using to hunt for your investment properties, so you can use these sites to your greatest advantage.

Additionally, it will enable you to represent yourself in real estate transactions, which will be beneficial for you in more ways than one. Becoming an agent will allow you to claim the referral commission anytime you buy a new property. My commission from being an agent has totaled over $10 million in the past eight years!

The other benefit of representing yourself in your real estate transactions is that at the end of the day, no one else is going to have your best interests in mind to the extent that you will.

Remember, a good player uses every possible advantage, and becoming a real estate agent is a great advantage in the building of your $100 million real estate portfolio.

Establish Your Credibility

You can probably tell by now that in order to maximize the Contrarian PlayBook strategy, you will need to work on an ongoing basis to become knowledgeable and stay informed. Establishing your credibility as a real estate investor should also be high on your list of priorities. While educating yourself is a big part of accomplishing this, there are other facets of your credibility that you should be aware of as well.

Personal Credibility

While financial credibility can be determined objectively, some aspects of credibility are more subjective in nature, such as the degree to which you come across as knowledgeable, stable, and trustworthy to the people you work with. In this regard, your best bet is to educate yourself as much as possible before you begin forging relationships with the industry professionals who will become valuable members of your real estate investment team. Once you've made your initial connections with these people, build your credibility with them by consistently living up to your word and following through on your commitments. Your good credibility will not be built overnight, but it is something to keep in mind and to prioritize from the get-go.

Financial Credibility

Your financial credibility is essential to your long-term success in real estate. It will grow with every deal you add to your buyer's resume, and in that respect, it too takes time to build.

From the very beginning though, your personal credit score will be the most fundamental indicator of financial credibility that you have. If you have poor credit, take steps to correct it right away–having good credit is essential if you want to qualify for financing, and financing is an absolutely critical part of any truly successful career in real estate.

There was a time in my life when I was up to my ears in credit card debt, but I never once defaulted on my payments. While many of my friends and family were advising me to file bankruptcy, I knew that if I wanted to become wealthy in this country, I needed to use the system. I paid 20 percent interest for over two years on my credit cards, sweating bullets all the while, but I knew that preserving my credit was a critical part of my long-term plan. In the end, I was right–having good credit has opened many doors for me, especially with lenders. Without my good credit, I never would have been able to build my real estate portfolio–or my wealth–to the degree that I have.

Final Thoughts

The information you collect and analyze through your research will definitely power you up, arming you with the facts you will need in order to determine if it is the right time to invest. As a contrarian, what will separate you from most other investors is that you will be making your decisions based on your own research, not deciding to buy or sell because the talking heads told you to. Making decisions based on findings from your own research takes cojones, but the rewards will be great!

Your strength as an investor is going to depend not only on your knowledge, but on your credibility as well. Unless you come across as both informed and reliable, you are not going to be taken seriously by the lenders, agents, brokers, and other industry professionals who can help you build your $100 million portfolio. Any steps you take to amp up these aspects of your game will pave the way for every deal you ever make!

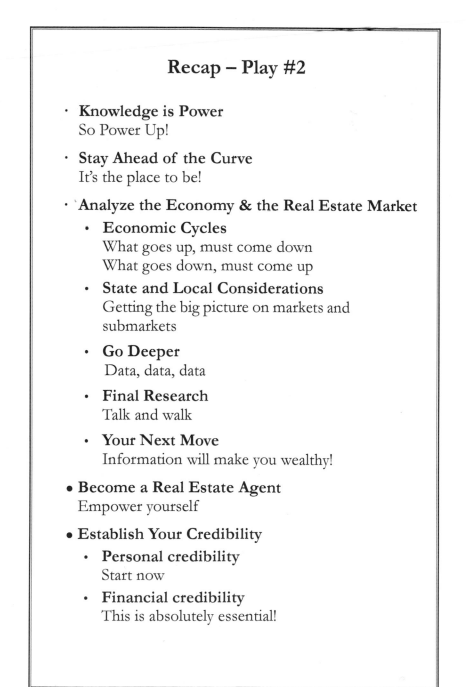

Recap – Play #2

- **Knowledge is Power**
  So Power Up!

- **Stay Ahead of the Curve**
  It's the place to be!

- **Analyze the Economy & the Real Estate Market**
  - **Economic Cycles**
    What goes up, must come down
    What goes down, must come up

  - **State and Local Considerations**
    Getting the big picture on markets and
    submarkets

  - **Go Deeper**
    Data, data, data

  - **Final Research**
    Talk and walk

  - **Your Next Move**
    Information will make you wealthy!

- **Become a Real Estate Agent**
  Empower yourself

- **Establish Your Credibility**
  - **Personal credibility**
    Start now

  - **Financial credibility**
    This is absolutely essential!

Play #3

Use Your Resources

Your Resources are Key

As you start out on the path to your $100 million real estate portfolio, your success will depend largely on the degree to which you recognize–and effectively use–the resources available to you. In real estate investment, your key resources are going to be the collective experience and knowledge of your "team members" (lenders, real estate agents, and other industry professionals you work with along the way), your financing options, and the unique tax considerations and benefits available to you as a real estate investor. By taking full advantage of these resources, you are adding fuel to your game.

Key Resource #1: Your Team

A big part of success in real estate investment is making full use of your team. If, as discussed in the last play, you come across as a knowledgeable and credible investor, your relationship with other real estate professionals will prosper. If you also maintain your connections with these professionals over time, they will see that you are a serious investor, which will further build your credibility. Before you know it, you will have a team of professionals you can trust and rely on. The more you cultivate these relationships, the more likely it is that your team members will bring good opportunities to you. On a contrarian's team, everybody wins! Essentially, your team members are your partners–or, as I like to call them, my "Board Members."

A note to new investors: Start your team now. Don't wait until you think you have more to offer them–give these professionals a chance to get in with you at the ground floor! Let them know that you have a dream and a strategy, and that you plan on building your $100 million portfolio from the ground up!

Banker(s) and Mortgage Broker(s)

The relationships you have with your lender(s) and/or broker(s) are probably the most valuable of all. When trying to jump through the hoops of financing, a banker or broker on your side will make a huge difference, especially if you have established your credibility to them. They can make your financing go very smoothly and that is invaluable.

Eventually it will serve you to deal with one lender as much as possible (I have been with Wells Fargo since 1992, and have had over $60 million in financing from them), but as a new investor it is advisable to reach out to several lenders. Doing so will give you some leverage. Make them compete against each other, and see who can offer you the best terms!

Real Estate (RE) Agent

Even after you get your real estate license, good RE agents are going to be essential members of your team, whether as agents or colleagues. RE agents will know (or have access to) the ins and outs of different areas within a city, and will be familiar with local demographics, schools, and crime statistics. If you haven't yet gotten licensed, an RE agent will have access to specific property information that the average person does not, such as detailed listing histories. With this information, a good RE Agent can definitely help you dodge some bullets.

Until you get your own RE license, a good agent will also be of help in completing the considerable amount of paperwork involved in real estate transactions, and will help you to devise and execute a good negotiation strategy.

Finding the RE agents that you want for your team is essential. There are lots of agents out there, so shop around! Find the agent(s) you truly connect with. You want to find agents who are genuinely interested in helping you with your goals, both short and long-term, rather than those that are just looking for their next commission. Look at the experience of the agent as well–it takes time for an agent to really get to know their market.

Tax Advisor

Real estate investors enjoy a number of tax benefits and considerations. A good tax advisor will help you to use these to your greatest advantage, making it possible for you to reach your financial goals much faster by maximizing the profitability of every one of your real estate transactions, and reinvesting the profits into new acquisitions.

Real Estate Attorney

For residential deals, a RE attorney is generally not needed, since the forms and contracts used are standardized and regulated by the Local Association of Realtors. For example, in California you have the California Association of Realtors (CAR). Also, most potential legal red flags will be brought to your attention by the title company and your lender. For commercial real estate transactions, a good RE attorney is worth the expense, because you will be dealing with larger stakes and more complicated, unique contracts. Furthermore, while agents and brokers often only get paid if the deal closes, and therefore might have their own agendas prioritized over yours, a real estate attorney's only loyalty will be to you and your best interests.

Property Inspector

When you buy a property, a thorough property inspection during the due diligence period of escrow will reveal the degree of deferred maintenance you will have to deal with if you buy the property. You can use any negative findings as reasons to request further price reductions from the seller. The more thorough and competent the inspector, the more leverage you will have during negotiations.

Contractors

Contractors are also important during the due diligence period. Once the property inspection is complete, you will need to know the costs of any necessary repairs or alterations. With commercial acquisitions it is imperative that you have several good general contractors give you estimates. Solid estimates will allow you to accurately assess your deferred maintenance, and negotiate accordingly.

Key Resource #2: Financing

Knowing the types (and amount) of financing that you qualify for will help you to narrow your focus when you are ready to begin actively looking for investment properties. Don't be afraid of debt in the process of building your portfolio. Not only is investing with borrowed funds nothing to be afraid of, it plays a very important role in being successful in real estate: It allows you to dramatically increase your profits by investing in assets that are far more valuable than what you might be able to afford by paying out of pocket.

In real estate investment, leveraging refers to using borrowed money to increase your profits. For example, let's say you have $100,000 in savings, and you use that to buy a $100,000 property outright. Assuming that real estate appreciates at the average rate of 7 percent annually, after one year your property will be worth $107,000; after two years, it will be worth $114,490; and after three years, it will be worth over $122,500.

Now let's imagine that instead of paying cash for a property valued at $100,000, you instead use that money as a down payment on a property worth $500,000. In a year, the property will be worth $535,000; in two, it will be worth $572,450; and in three, its value will have climbed to a little over $612,500.

Even if you only own the property for a year, through leveraging your way into a more valuable investment you will have increased your profits by $28,000. In two years, you will have increased them by $57,960. By the end of the third year, your leverage will have increased your profits by $90,000. You will, of course, need to factor in the cost of interest on the loan, but even then you will be looking at a greatly enhanced bottom line, thanks to the effective use of leverage.

Property Bought	Year 1 Value	Year 2 Value	Year 3 Value
$100,000 property	$107,000	$114, 490	$122,500
$500,000 property	$535,000	$572,450	$612,500

Seen another way:

Property Bought	3 year Gain	Return (%)
$100,000 property	22,500	22.5%
$500,000 property	112,500	>100%

Notes:
Based on a 7% appreciation rate per year
Does not take interest and loan cost into consideration

If you have already achieved the kind of wealth that would allow you to pay cash for more valuable assets, leveraging can prevent you from tying up large portions of your liquidity–and the more liquidity you have, the faster you can grow your portfolio by buying more property! If you choose your investment properties wisely, it can be very beneficial to take on some debt in the process–provided the property you are buying has enough income to carry the debt service.

Mortgages

There are two basic types of mortgages: Adjustable and fixed. Adjustable rate mortgages are appealing because they often offer lower initial rates, but since the interest can vary significantly over the life of the loan, you could eventually find yourself paying a much higher interest rate. With the fixed rate mortgage, the interest rate is locked in, which can provide a certain security. Generally, you want to stay away from any mortgage with less than five years fixed.

Mortgages are a big topic all their own. In fact, there are books written on just mortgages. Talk to your banker or mortgage broker about the best choice for you at any given time.

FHA Loans

If the only thing preventing you from qualifying for financing is not having savings for a down payment, then an FHA (Federal Housing Administration) government loan program might be a good option for you to pursue. FHA loans are exclusively for first-time home buyers. FHA loans can be used for any owner-occupied residential property of four units or less, with the exception of some condominiums (you can go to the FHA website for further information on their various programs).

There are pros and cons to FHA loans. On the plus side, they have a very low minimum down payment requirement (as low as 3.5 percent), and offer a variety of low and fixed interest options for the first time home buyer, including individuals with lower income. An FHA loan is a great stepping stone for someone with limited savings, and provides an opportunity to build equity. The down side is that you need to pay for PMI (premium mortgage insurance) each month, which averages between $80 and $200 per month. Also, borrowing 100 percent (or close to it, anyway) carries increased risk.

If you have the money for a larger down payment, I wouldn't recommend the FHA loan. A non-FHA down payment is usually 10-20 percent for properties with four units or less, and the larger your down payment, the smaller your monthly payments. Cash flow is a major consideration with any investment; if borrowing nearly 100 percent puts you at a negative cash flow, it's not going to help you. Whether you end up going the FHA route or not, if you are a first-time buyer it is good to be aware that it is an option. Your options are resources.

I purchased my first home in 1997, using FHA financing with 3 percent down. It was a six-bedroom, bank-owned (REO) home that had previously sold for $200,000. I bought it for $142,000 and sold it a year later for $220,000, realizing a gain of almost $80,000! Given my financial situation at the time, I could not have done this without FHA financing.

VA Loans

A VA loan is a zero down financing option for veterans, active-duty service members, and spouses of individuals killed in the line of duty. If you qualify for this type of financing, it is a tremendous resource, and unlike FHA it is not strictly for first-time home buyers. The same risks of borrowing 100 percent still apply, and eligibility is not guaranteed based on service, but it is worth looking into if you think you might qualify.

Refinancing

If you own your own home, but don't have money for a down payment on the purchase of an income property, you should explore your refinancing options. "Cashing out," or drawing a second mortgage or line of credit against one of your properties in order to acquire another, is a perfect example of making your properties work for you—and making your properties work for you is a cornerstone of the Contrarian PlayBook strategy! Since all properties perform differently, it can be beneficial in certain market conditions to use the leverage on one to pay off another, or to buy more properties. (Keep in mind that both the FHA and VA offer home refinance loans.)

Seller Financing

This is my favorite type of financing. It usually has the lowest loan costs and quickest processing time, and is very convenient and practical for all involved. Sellers are often motivated to provide this type of financing because it provides them with a consistent cash flow while freeing them from the hassles of real estate management. In more cases than not, you will be able to negotiate more favorable terms with a seller than with a traditional bank. Finally, seller financing can mean a quick closing, which is great for everyone involved.

When I bought my first commercial property the seller offered to carry the note. I was thrilled to be able to negotiate the price and the interest rate at the same time. I ended up with a no-cost, very low interest loan, fully amortized over ten years. The loan itself was a huge value: The interest rate was well below the market rate of 7.5 percent, and I was able to close the deal quickly because there was no third-party (bank) involvement. Of the three properties that the real estate agent presented to me, this is the one I took, and the seller financing was a large factor in my decision.

On the other end of this, seller financing is not something I offer when selling. I don't want my money tied up in that way, as the 6-10 percent return I could expect from the interest on the loan doesn't measure up to the average return on my investments.

Your Cash

In later plays you will learn that there are circumstances under which paying cash for a property will work to your advantage—but this doesn't really apply until you have the increased liquidity afforded by a certain level of wealth. Until you achieve that level of prosperity, securing financing is going to be necessary.

That being said, when you do have the liquidity to pay cash for a property, it can be very effective in securing the best possible deal. It can also come in very handy in recessions, when banks tighten their lending restrictions.

Key Resource #3:
Tax Benefits & Considerations

Whole books have been written on the various tax benefits and considerations available to real estate investors. It is beyond the scope of this book to explore these in any great detail, but being aware of these options and utilizing them effectively will greatly increase your return on investment (ROI) as you grow your portfolio. The following is intended to serve as a brief overview.

1031 Exchange

The term "1031 exchange" references Section 1031 of the Internal Revenue Code. As it pertains to real estate, Section 1031 allows you to defer paying tax on capital gains from the sale of an investment property by reinvesting those proceeds into another like-kind investment property of equal or greater value. As long as you keep reinvesting, you can potentially avoid paying taxes on your capital gains.

You should be aware that by using 1031 exchange you also defer any capital losses you would otherwise have claimed on your taxes. Another thing to consider is that the replacement property (the property in which you reinvest the proceeds from a sale) must be identified within 45 days of closing escrow on the first property, and acquired within 180 days.

I have used 1031 exchange throughout my career in real estate, and it has been a major factor in the speed—and profitability—with which I've grown my own portfolio. By pushing me to keep buying, it pushed me to my wealth! It is a powerful motivator to never stop looking for new opportunities, and to keep your head in the game!

Depreciation

In real estate, depreciation refers to the gradual loss of value of a building due to normal wear and tear. It is calculated off the assessed value of the building, and is itemized as an expense on your income taxes. Itemizing depreciation as an expense reduces your taxable income, and therefore increases your cash flow. With an income property, you can also deduct the depreciation of any capital improvements you make to the building.

Depreciation is normally calculated on a 27.5-year basis for residential income properties, and a 39-year basis for commercial income properties; however, for commercial properties it is possible to accelerate the rate of depreciation through a process called cost segregation.

Cost Segregation

Cost segregation can shorten the basis for calculating depreciation, thereby accelerating your timetable, reducing your taxable income, and increasing your cash flow in the short term.

To put it as simply as possible, cost segregation involves separating out tenant improvements from real property and shortening their depreciation time. Cost segregation studies are not cheap, but they can yield large returns, and can shorten the time frame for calculating depreciation from 39 years to as little as 5 years. This strategy often pays for itself in the first few months by reducing your income tax liability, which in turn increases your cash flow.

Final Thoughts

You can have access to all the resources in the world, but what will ultimately decide your success as a real estate investor is how you use them. Be resourceful with your resources! Continue to use them as you build your portfolio and accumulate wealth. You will never be too wealthy to benefit from the effective use of your resources, from the collective expertise of your team members, to your many financing options, to the various tax benefits and considerations available to you as a real estate investor.

Recap – Play #3

- **Your Resources are Key**
  Use all of them

- **Key Resource #1: Your Team**
  Let your team help you–it's win-win
  for everyone

  - **Banker(s) & Mortgage Broker(s)**
  - **Real Estate Agent**
  - **Tax Advisor**
  - **Real Estate Attorney**
  - **Property Inspector**
  - **Contractors**

- **Key Resource #2: Financing**
  Don't be afraid of debt

  - **Mortgages**
  - **FHA Loans**
  - **VA Loans**
  - **Refinancing**
  - **Seller Financing**
  - **Your Cash**

- **Key Resource #3: Tax Benefits**
  Enjoy the benefits!

  - **1031 Exchange**
  - **Depreciation**
  - **Cost Segregation**

MAKE YOUR MONEY ON THE BUY

DO IT!

While you know I value big dreams, they only hang out in the clouds until you take action. I wrote this book for those of you who are ready to take action, and get in the game. You are reading this playbook because you are ready to do what it takes to turn your dreams into realities.

At this stage, many new investors are often unsure of how to start acting on the goals they have set for themselves. Keep in mind that taking action doesn't have to mean rushing out to make your first buys. In many cases, even actions that seem inconsequential on the surface can end up having a powerful impact on your life and career. The following story explains how I made my first million dollars, and is a good illustration of how even the smallest action can produce big results.

My First Million Dollar Profit

Early on in my real estate investment career, I was eyeing this small block of commercial property, which consisted of a 10,000 square foot building. I drove by it everyday, as it was across the street from my P.O. Box. It was closed down for several years, and I couldn't seem to get any information on it. One day, I saw a man with a locksmith's van in the parking lot of the property. Assuming that this meant that the ownership had changed hands, I drove over to find out if he was the new owner. He wasn't, but I found out he worked for a bank that had just taken it back through a trustee sale (foreclosure) a couple of days before.

My heart started to pound faster–this was my golden opportunity! He gave me the name of the real estate agent who was going to handle the property, and as soon as I left the parking lot I called the agent. He did not yet know anything about the building, but I insisted that he was going to get the listing. He agreed to meet with me the next day.

This property was very unique, and a very high-demand asset. The traffic count on the street was thousands of cars per day and there were rarely vacancies on this street, making it a true gem. All I had to do was tie up the deal before it hit the market.

After meeting with the broker I knew that if I was going to get this building, I had to give him as much incentive as I could. I told him that since I myself was a real estate broker, I was willing to forfeit my commission to him if he would fight for me and get the bank to take my offer. Remember that this was a foreclosure, so the listing price was what the bank owed on it, which was $825,000.

My first offer was $530,000, which the listing broker hesitated to write. I anticipated that the bank, as with any bank, would want to get this negative asset off their balance sheets. After all, banks are not in the business of managing real estate; they are in the business of lending money. So when the bank countered my initial offer at $750,000, my response was $600,000. In the end, we settled on $675,000 with a 30-day closing. The thing was, I only had a few thousand dollars!

I knew this was my big break—if I could just tie it up for now, then I could raise the funds to purchase it. I gave them a $10,000 deposit and we proceeded to open escrow. Because all of my money was tied up in two homes and a shopping center, that $10,000 was all I had—and I took it from my personal line of credit!

I now had to find a lender who could give me the loan in less than 30 days. During this time I also received the title report from the bank as part of the requirements per our purchase contract. While reviewing the title report I noticed a substandard lien by the city, which indicated that the structure of the building had been altered without permits, and that it no longer met the building standards as a result. It was a huge red flag, but it was also a blessing in disguise for me, because it bought me time. I knew the seller would be required to clear all liens from the property by closing. I now had a way to extend the closing of escrow.

I immediately went to the city to get more information. I requested an inspection, which revealed that the prior owner had removed a bearing wall without properly reinforcing the structure, making the building unsafe. I told the bank that it needed to be corrected since I could neither obtain financing nor record title to my name with the lien on it. Per the purchase contract, the bank had to deliver me a property with a clean title, so they agreed to fix it.

Fixing it would require several months, and during this time I applied for an SBA loan for the purchase of the building. After a few months I was informed that the bank was canceling the sale because the city was now requiring the building to be earthquake retro-fitted, and the parking and landscaping to be brought up to code. This was hundreds of thousands of dollars in improvements and could easily take a year, if not more. Knowing the price they had agreed to was a significant discount to its current value, the bank wanted to cancel their contract with me and sell at a much higher price after they had made all the improvements—but I wasn't going to let them get away with that!

After a short legal battle, the bank agreed to continue with the sale, and on top of that they gave me $67,000 for the landscaping! The bank spent over $300,000 on the improvements the city required. I had my SBA loan ready, and due to my great credit I was able to use my home to get a home equity line of credit for the down payment. I ended up purchasing the property with $67,000 down.

It took me four months to remodel it, and one month to sell it–for $1,600,000!

You can imagine the feeling I had when the money was wired to my bank. I was a millionaire! I was 29 years old and I had realized just how much I loved the real estate game. By taking a simple action of driving across the street one day, I set my first million dollar deal in motion. Then I continued to activate the path it opened, and in the end, I made a lot of money on the buy!

Play #4

Select Your
Property Type:
Residential

Your Investment Choices

Now that you're ready to jump into the game, your first step in finding the right investment is to decide which type of property is the best fit for you and your current circumstances. In this play, we are going to be looking at three residential property types: The condominium, the single family residence, and the 2-4 unit apartment complex. Each type has its own characteristics, and its own set of pros and cons to consider.

If you are an experienced investor with several years' experience and multiple residential income properties already in your portfolio, you may want to jump to Plays #6 and #7, which discuss commercial properties.

If you are a new investor, you are in the right place! I recommend that you begin building your portfolio with residential properties, because the typical commercial real estate deal is more complex and involves a greater degree of due diligence. Also, most commercial properties come at a much higher price point and require a 25-40 percent down payment, making them unrealistic first buys for most beginning investors. Take my advice, and get some experience under your belt with residential properties first.

There are lots of reasons why the residential market is an ideal place to start building a real estate portfolio. First of all, it offers viable investment opportunities for people of most income levels. Of all the various types of real estate, residential is the least risky and has the highest demand—after all, people need a roof over their heads, and the population is growing! Starting with residential will allow you to gain experience with various aspects of the investment process—from dealing with lenders to negotiating with sellers, from securing financing to property management—in a smaller-scale, more hands-on environment.

Residential Property Types

The three types of properties covered in this section are the condominium, the single family residence, and the 2-4 unit apartment complex.

Owner Occupied v. Non-Owner Occupied

If you do not yet own your own home, you should plan on living in the first residential property you buy. Owner-occupied (O.O.) properties are subject to far less stringent financing requirements than are non-owner occupied (N.O.O.) properties. Loans for N.O.O. properties are called "investor loans," and the properties you buy with them are ineligible for many of the tax benefits and financing perks available to owner-occupied home loan applicants. If you go the N.O.O. route, be prepared to pay a larger down payment and higher interest rates and fees.

Also consider that even if you plan on renting out the property, it is still a residential loan. As such, lenders are not going to base their financing on the income the property would provide, but rather on your income. Most will require that you have cash reserves to cover six months of mortgage payments. These N.O.O. mortgages carry a heightened risk for the lender, because people are more likely to default on an investment property than on a personal residence–so if you go the N.O.O. route, be prepared to pay more to offset this risk.

Condominium: Pros & Cons

Pros:

The condo has the lowest price point of all residential property types, making it the most affordable option to the new investor with limited resources. In addition, some condos qualify for FHA or VA financing (provided, of course, that you intend to make it your primary residence, and that you meet the other requirements), so depending on your circumstances you can buy one with as little as 0-3.5 percent down.

Another positive aspect of condo ownership is that it is relatively hassle-free; property maintenance is largely taken care of by your Home Owner's Association (HOA) management, so you will not have to worry about the upkeep of the building exterior, common areas, roof, and grounds.

Cons:

As the owner of a condo you will need to pay regular dues to your HOA. I just mentioned that from a maintenance perspective, your HOA can make your life easier. That said, poor HOA management can not only complicate your life, but cost you money as well. If your HOA mismanages its funds, your monthly dues could go up substantially.

If you do decide that a condo would be your best option as a first buy, you should request basic financial information from the complex's HOA, including their current year budget, how much they have in the way of reserves, and the cost of any major upcoming repairs. This will give you an idea of how well-run the HOA is in that particular complex.

As a condo owner you will also have the added complication of sharing walls with people who have as much—or more—of a stake in the property as you do. This increases the likelihood of conflict between the residents, which has been known to result in lawsuits. Lawsuits and any pending claims associated with them will devalue your property, whether you are directly involved or not.

Another potential downside to condo ownership is that you will have to abide by the complex's Covenants, Conditions & Restrictions (CC&Rs), which govern how the complex is run.

CC&Rs typically impose far-reaching regulations on their members, dealing with everything from parking, exterior remodel, use restrictions, and behavior in the common areas.

Furthermore, from a return on investment perspective, condos do not offer the best rate of return when compared to other residential properties. A condo also does not have as much of an upside in future value as other residential properties, meaning that it provides fewer opportunities for you to add value, and adding value is one of the best ways to increase your ROI when it comes time to sell.

Last but not least, the condo typically appreciates at a slower rate than its residential income counterparts—and rate of appreciation is a significant factor with any investment property.

There are a number of potential downsides to the condo as an investment. Overall, I only recommend investing in a condominium if it is the only type of residential property you can realistically obtain financing for.

Single Family Residence (SFR): Pros & Cons

Pros:

The single family residence is the second most affordable type of property in the residential market. It shares many of the same financing perks of the condo, in that it qualifies for lower-down options such as the FHA and VA loans—but even if you do not qualify for the FHA/VA options, the down payment for a SFR with a standard loan can be as low as ten percent.

Unlike the condo, the single family residence is not typically burdened with restrictions on parking and exterior remodeling. The SFR owner has much more control over the property, its appearance, and how it is run. As a result, the SFR owner enjoys the added benefit of pride of ownership–and if you don't know from personal experience already, you are about to find out that pride of ownership is one of the greatest things about being a real estate investor!

SFRs also provide you with a far greater upside in terms of adding value. You will have the freedom to increase the value of the property in a number of ways, with methods as involved as structural expansion (adding square footage) and as basic as painting the exterior or adding landscaping.

Cons:

The biggest downside of the SFR is that it offers less cash flow when compared with small residential income properties. If you live in it yourself, you will be paying the debt service out of pocket, as it will not be providing you with any income. While you do have the option of renting it out (provided you didn't finance with FHA or VA, which both require that it be your primary residence), it carries more risk than a property with multiple units. Renting out your SFR could pay for a large percentage–if not all–of your mortgage payment, but if your tenant defaults on rent, or leaves unexpectedly, it would cost you 100 percent of the property's income, leaving you to foot 100 percent of the expenses until you are able to fill it again. In this way, the SFR has a higher vacancy loss risk than a multi-unit property.

Another downside to the SFR is that it appreciates (much like the condo) at a slower rate than residential income properties.

Overall, I would recommend the SFR over the condo as an entry-level investment, assuming it fits your price point. That said, check out all the pros of the 2-4 Plex!

2-4 Plex: Pros & Cons

Pros:

In my experience, the 2-4 unit complex is the ideal investment for someone who is just getting started in real estate and has the resources for the down payment. Because it has fewer than 5 units, it still qualifies for FHA/VA financing, as long as you plan to live in one of the units. If you don't qualify for either one of these options, you can still purchase it with a residential loan, which carries a smaller minimum down payment and a lower interest rate than a commercial loan.

One of the greatest benefits of the 2-4 plex is that it qualifies for residential financing while generating a steady stream of rental income for you as the owner. Even if you live in one of the units, the income from the remaining units will pay for much, if not all, of your mortgage expense. By living in one of the units, you are also eligible for the full spectrum of tax deductions that can be applied towards owner-occupied residential properties.

The 2-4 plex also has a lower vacancy loss risk than the SFR or condo. Imagine that you purchase a 4 plex and occupy one of the units yourself. If a tenant defaults on rent or leaves without warning, you are only losing one third of your total rental income, vs. losing 100 percent from the same scenario with a condo or SFR.

Last but not least, the value of a multi-unit residential property also appreciates at a higher rate than the condo or SFR, which, as I said before, is a very important factor in selecting an investment property.

The 2-4 plex really is the ideal first investment property, provided you can afford the down payment and qualify for a loan. A number of years ago, I advised one of my old friends–who had been renting his home, and had no savings aside from the $15,000 his wife had in her 401k–to buy a 4 plex with FHA financing, using the 401k as a down payment.

I found them a great deal on a 4 plex. They lived in one unit, and the rental income from the other units covered their mortgage in full! I sold that property for them after a year, and over the next decade I invested their proceeds from that first 4 plex, and rolled it into a net worth of over $1.5 million!

Cons:

A multi-unit property is going to be more management intensive and require more maintenance than a condo or SFR, and therefore you can expect to have higher operating expenses. These expenses can be offset, at least in part, by living onsite and managing the property yourself.

The only other downside of the 2-4 plex is that the rental rates provide less of an upside when compared to commercial income property, meaning that there is less potential to increase the operational income (and therefore the value of the asset) by significantly raising the rental rates.

Final Thoughts

I began this section by encouraging you to begin building your portfolio with residential properties, and transitioning to commercial properties when you have some experience under your belt. Eventually, you will need to make the leap to commercial if you want to make the most of my investment strategy and build your portfolio to the $100 million mark. That being said, it is only advisable to make this transition when you feel confident about doing so. Until then, gain experience with the various aspects of being a landlord in the residential arena, where the risk, and the stakes, are lower.

Now that you have a basic understanding of the pros and cons of the various types of residential properties, you are in a good position to begin a more focused search for whichever one best fits your current circumstances. The important thing is to get your investment portfolio started.

In Play #5 I will give you all the criteria you will need as you begin your search for the right residential property. Use the criteria to "pick a winner!"

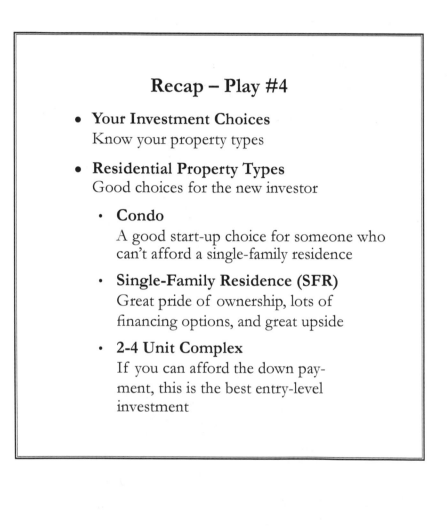

Recap – Play #4

- **Your Investment Choices**
  Know your property types

- **Residential Property Types**
  Good choices for the new investor

  - **Condo**
    A good start-up choice for someone who can't afford a single-family residence

  - **Single-Family Residence (SFR)**
    Great pride of ownership, lots of financing options, and great upside

  - **2-4 Unit Complex**
    If you can afford the down payment, this is the best entry-level investment

Play #5

Pick a Winner: Residential

The Search is On!

Now that you have selected your residential property type, the search for the winning property begins! Finding the right property—one that will make you money on the buy—is a dynamic process with several distinct steps. First, you will define your market: The general geographical area in which you will be looking. Next, you will define your submarket, the neighborhood which holds the best investment opportunities. Finally, you will use your resources to pick a winning property in your submarket, according to the Contrarian PlayBook's criteria. All of this will put you on the path to your $100 million real estate portfolio!

Define Your Market

Residential property investments should be kept relatively local, as they can be very management intensive. If you are a new investor, I absolutely advise you to keep your first buys in your own backyard—within a 5-20 mile radius of your home or place of employment.

A property reasonably close to your job/office will be helpful in securing the more favorable financing terms that are available for owner-occupied property. If you apply for financing for a property that is far away from your job, your lender may not believe that you are actually going to live there. Even if you intend to rent the property out, I would still advise you to find a property close to where you live/work because it will make it easier for you to be a hands-on landlord.

Within the 5-20 mile radius of your home or workplace, you will likely have at least one county, and multiple cities, to research. When I research a housing market, the first thing I do is go online. As you learned in Play #2, there are several steps involved in the thorough research of a market or submarket. Remember that Zillow is a fantastic site for a broad spectrum of information on any particular state or city economy, and even gives you detailed information about specific neighborhoods within a city! Also remember not to restrict your research to just "real estate information." Since so many factors affect a market or submarket's economy, check out local news and community information too.

Research Your Submarkets

Within your local market, some areas (submarkets) are going to offer you better chances of finding residential properties that will make you money on the buy. For instance, there are times when an overall market may be heading up, but a submarket–a particular city or neighborhood–is lagging behind, and therefore still offers good investment opportunities.

Keep in mind that as a contrarian, you are not looking for your dream home–you are looking for a good investment, a property that you will be able to sell at a profit down the line. With this in mind, you need to be sure to buy a property that is located in a fluid area–in other words, an area with high demand.

In assessing demand, you will be weighing a variety of statistical information, including population growth (historical and projected), employment data, and area demographics. A winning property should be in a well-populated submarket with projected population growth, as well as an economically diverse population base and ample employment opportunities. Keep in mind that the right property also has to be one that fits your financial circumstances and your risk tolerance, so you will need to factor in these considerations.

Sometimes, the process of studying the submarkets along these lines will yield a clear stand-out among them, but it's very possible that you will find several submarkets that look promising and provide you with viable investment opportunities. When this is the case, visit them all! You have nothing to lose. Get that "feet on the ground" insight we talked about in Play #2. Talk with your team about your options, and get their input. Last but not least, use the criteria we're about to cover–they will give you a huge advantage when it comes to picking a winning property!

Criteria for Residential Property

When searching for the right property, I use a very specific set of criteria to determine whether or not it is a wise investment. Sticking to these criteria has been a critical part of my success in real estate investment. Follow them as I have, and you will be making money on the buy in no time!

The criteria below are for residential properties, and are divided into two segments: The first outlines the criteria for the condo/SFR and the second contains additional criteria for the 2-4 plex. As you read, keep in mind that no matter what type of property you are looking for, your job is to identify the property that makes the best investment.

Sticking with the criteria will ensure that you buy a property that will be easy to sell at a profit down the line; straying from them could result in you buying a property that you get stuck with for the long haul. For any investor, but particularly for the first-time buyer with limited resources, making a wise investment is critical. It could take years to recover from a misstep in these early stages—so take your time, follow the criteria, and wait for the right property!

Criteria for the Right Single Family Residence and Condominium

Criterion #1: Priced at a Discount

The right property of any kind is always, and without exception, priced at a discount—after all, that is how you make your money on the buy! In order to identify a good deal, you will need to look at the price per square foot amongst like properties in your submarket. The price per square foot (or "price per pound," as I call it) is the most readily apparent indicator of a discounted property.

In order to find out if a property is discounted, you'll need to analyze its list price per square foot against both the current list prices and recent sales prices of other like properties, also referred to as comps. Comps (short for comparables) are properties similar in type and size, located in the same neighborhood. Looking at comps is the quickest way to single out the discounted properties in any given submarket.

Beyond the price per pound, you should also keep an eye out for distressed sales, such as foreclosures, or properties with a desperate seller. One of the ways to identify the latter is by looking at the listing history for multiple price reductions. You can find this information on MLS sites by inputting the address and pulling up the canceled/expired/sold category for the last three years. Also, read the real estate agent comments on the MLS listing. It often states "Distressed" or "Seller Must Sell Fast" or "Sellers Very Motivated."

There are a number of common seller circumstances that result in distressed property sales, ranging from foreclosure to death to divorce. Where death is the cause, the resulting sale of the property is referred to as a probate sale. While there are remarkable discounts to be found in the probate market, you will need to find out if someone physically died in the house, as this is something you will be legally obligated to disclose to any potential buyer in the future. A death on the property instantly reduces your buyer's audience—especially if the death was crime-related—so as a general rule it's good to avoid scenarios like these when looking for the right condo or SFR.

Auctions are also to be avoided, both because you will be competing against a larger number of potential buyers and because you will be making decisions in an accelerated time frame, which makes it difficult to do your due diligence. When it's a good time to buy there will be an abundance of discounted properties to be found, so you won't need to rely on auctions.

Criterion #2: Good Location

To narrow the definition of a good location within a defined submarket, you will need to consider a number of factors. One of these factors would be the local crime statistics. Usually it isn't good for a property to be next to or across from a high school, as this often correlates to an increase in petty crime. Whether it is close to a high school or not, it is always a good idea for you to call the local police department, let them know that you are looking to move to the area, and ask to speak with someone who can answer your questions regarding the area crime statistics. They will patch you through to someone who knows all of the "hot spots," the areas with the highest criminal activity—and therefore the areas you should avoid when looking for the right investment property.

Too close to a freeway isn't good for residential property either, because of the noise factor. If you make the mistake of buying too close to a freeway, it will be much harder to sell in the future. If the neighborhood is too noisy, future buyers won't even want to come in the front door to look at it—and since you're buying as an investment, you always need to have the future buyers in mind. Ideally, the right residential property should be located on a cul-de-sac or very quiet street.

Undesirable location can't be changed, no matter what you do, so make sure the location is good. In addition to calling the police department, find an agent who has worked in that neighborhood, tell them you're in the market for a condo or SFR, and ask for their opinion on where you should focus your search.

Criterion #3: Good Lot Size

Like location, lot size is not a characteristic that you have any control over—what you see is what you get! After you've compared like properties based on price per square foot and location, lot size is the next point of comparison. The larger the lot, the better the resale value–period. Obviously, "good" is a relative term as it applies to lot size, based on the average lot size of comps in your submarket.

Criterion #4: Presents an Upside

With a condo or house as a first buy, there are two ways in which you can make money: The first is on the direction of the market, and the second is going to be through the value you create by making cosmetic improvements to the property. As a contrarian, you should know by now that buying any property based solely on the direction of the market is classic speculative investment, which is never a good idea!

With that in mind, when you're comparing properties based on price per square foot, location and lot size you should also be looking for the property with the best upside–in other words, the property that provides you with the most opportunity to increase the value through cosmetic improvements. Steer clear of the biggest, most beautiful home on the block. Instead, look for a medium-sized home that looks a little rough around the edges and needs a little TLC. This presents an opportunity to add value in a number of ways, which can be as basic as painting and landscaping and as involved as adding square footage.

Don't look for the place that you would want to live forever–remember, this is not about finding your dream home! In the process of picking a winner, remember that the right property probably won't look like much of a winner at all. Look for the asset that comes at the right price, and comes with plenty of built-in room for improvement. Anything that looks rundown on the outside is something you will learn to see as an upside, a potential to increase the property's value, thereby maximizing your profits when you sell it to someone else in the future. Furthermore, anything that looks bad (i.e. ugly carpeting, or tacky paint colors) has probably been factored into a discounted listing price, or can be used to negotiate further discounts in escrow—or both!

Additional Criteria for the Right 2-4 Plex

When searching for a 2-4 plex, you will use all of the same criteria as you would for a condo or single family residence; below are some additional criteria that are specific to small residential income properties.

Criterion # 1: Below Market Rents

Foreclosures on residential income properties are rare, as they have built-in income with which to carry the basic expenses, but that's not to say that you can't find discounted and/or distressed 2-4 plexes. More often than not, these discounted and/or distressed residential income properties will offer an opportunity to add value. In the small residential income market, these sales often involve a landlord who hasn't made improvements in a long time, and consequently hasn't raised rents significantly in years; this creates the perfect opportunity for you to add value by making improvements and raising the rents gradually. For this reason, I don't recommend investing in these types of properties in rent-controlled areas, as rent control would severely limit the property's upside potential.

Criterion # 2: Good Unit Mix

Unit mix plays an important role in the selection of the right small residential income properties. A family usually won't move into a 1 bedroom unit, but would be willing to pay more per month to live in a 2 bedroom, because you rent per room. Most buyers won't want to buy a 4-plex that has only 1 bedrooms or studios in the mix, both because they command less rent and because they have a higher tenant rollover rate. When it comes to both rental revenues and tenant rollover, 2 bedroom/1 bath units are preferable.

Remember that even if you are going to be residing in your 2-4 plex you are still buying this property as an investment, so the ease with which you can sell it in the future is essential. For this reason, having a good unit mix is key.

Criterion #3: Low Crime Area

Just like with a condo or SFR, being located in a low crime area is very important for a small residential property, partly for its future salability and partly because it will spare you a great deal of stress as a landlord. A multi-unit property is the cheapest residential entry for a family, so you're going to be dealing largely with lower income tenants. This means that you need to be sure you're not in a high crime area. If the crime is bad, you will have trouble attracting good tenants. Misery loves company, and trouble attracts trouble.

A few years into my real estate investment career I bought an REO 4-plex in Anaheim, in a tough neighborhood. I knew it was a high crime area, but I got it for an incredible price. I ended up making $100,000 in a year with 20 percent down, but during that year I had a lot of trouble with the tenants. I took that risk after I had a good deal of experience under my belt, but I wouldn't recommend it for a new investor. When you are looking for residential income properties, go through the same process you would with a condo or SFR: Call the police department. They will be able to tell you if there are general areas or even particular streets that they have recurring issues with, which will help you make an informed choice.

Find the Right Residential Property

Now that you've defined your submarket and know how to identify a winning property, you need to know how and where to start your search! In the search for the right residential property, your two key resources are going to be MLS sites and the collective experience of your team members.

A good first step is to go online to multi-listing service (MLS) websites. Since you are looking at residential properties, you will be using your local MLS site (unlike commercial real estate, there is no nationwide MLS site for residential property). Search for the properties in your submarket(s) that fit your parameters, including the criteria we just covered.

When using MLS sites, you will be asked to select your property type, geographical area (typically definable by zip code), size, and price range. Keep in mind that you might have many options to choose from, but you can start by entering in the basics and further narrowing it down according to the criteria. The MLS sites will also provide you with detailed listing histories, as well as both current and historical sales information for comps in the area (remember that some of this information will only be available to you once you get your real estate license). This data will help you to contextualize the property listings that pique your interest, so you will be able to better judge whether or not they are worth pursuing. I always look at the 5 year sales history for comps in a given area. Not only does it help you to determine whether or not you've found a winning property, it also helps you to judge whether it's a good time to invest in that submarket, in terms of where it is in its economic cycle.

You can also check with the real estate agent(s) who you have worked or talked with in the past. See if they know of any properties on the market that might be up your alley. If you have a good relationship with your bank, check with them and see if they have any foreclosures that they want to get off their books.

Final Thoughts

The search for the right residential property is an involved and interesting process, which needs to be approached from a variety of angles. Luckily, there is a wealth of information to be found online, literally at your fingertips! Add the collective knowledge of your team members, and you will be able to gather all the information you need about the real estate market in your area, and select the submarket that presents the best opportunities. You will then be able to find a property within that submarket that will make you money on the buy, bringing you one step closer to your $100 million real estate portfolio! From this point on, each deal you make in the residential market will strengthen your knowledgeability, credibility, and confidence, as well as your relationship with your team—all of which will be invaluable when you make the transition to the commercial property market.

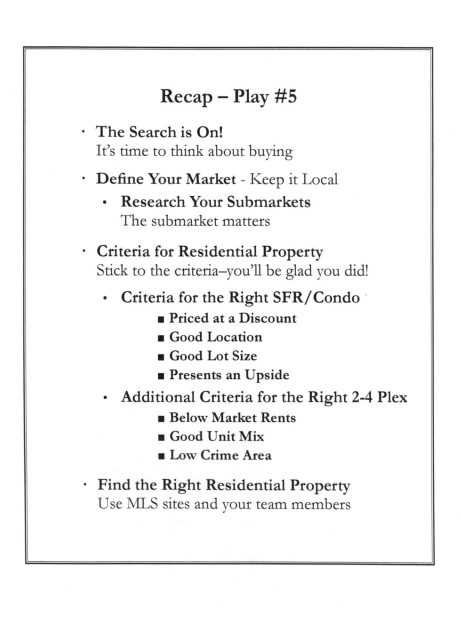

Recap – Play #5

- **The Search is On!**
  It's time to think about buying

- **Define Your Market** - Keep it Local
  - **Research Your Submarkets**
    The submarket matters

- **Criteria for Residential Property**
  Stick to the criteria–you'll be glad you did!
  - **Criteria for the Right SFR/Condo**
    - **Priced at a Discount**
    - **Good Location**
    - **Good Lot Size**
    - **Presents an Upside**
  - **Additional Criteria for the Right 2-4 Plex**
    - **Below Market Rents**
    - **Good Unit Mix**
    - **Low Crime Area**

- **Find the Right Residential Property**
  Use MLS sites and your team members

Play #6

Select Your Property Type: Commercial

Shift to Commercial Properties

In order to make the most of the Contrarian PlayBook strategy, you will, at some point, need to make the switch to commercial investment property. With commercial income property you are talking about more dollars per tenant and better opportunities. I'm not saying that it's impossible to build significant wealth through residential real estate alone, but it will take you far longer, and you will need to buy and sell a great many more properties. Residential properties are also much more management intensive. So the question you might ask yourself is: "Why chase ten smaller fish when I can catch a few big ones?"

I also want to reiterate that it is important not to rush into buying commercial properties if you are a new or part-time investor. It took me 15 years to move from residential to high rise office buildings. Admittedly, my portfolio included smaller commercial properties from the beginning, but in this case I am advising you to do as I say, not as I did!

Commercial Property Types

The following is an overview of four different commercial property types–apartment building, office, industrial, and retail–and the pros and cons of each.

Apartment Building: Pros & Cons

Note: Since the apartment building may be a transitional property type for the real estate investor moving from residential to commercial properties, I have included points of comparison with the residential property types as well.

Pros:

While apartment buildings with five or more units are classified as commercial properties, you are still dealing with residential tenants. In comparison to 2-4 plexes, apartment buildings in the same city will usually generate higher rental income per square foot, and therefore a larger cash flow. In addition, your return will be higher because you will have been required to put significantly more money down.

When compared with other commercial property types, one of the perks of apartment buildings is that they carry substantially less tenant loss risk because the vacancies are easier to fill. This is attributable to the fact that housing remains in high demand in any economy.

This is not to say that tenants are less likely to leave, only that you will have an easier time finding new tenants. It is important not to confuse tenant loss risk with tenant rollover. Tenant rollover is listed below as one of the downsides of apartment buildings, and is actually higher with apartment buildings than it is with other types of commercial property.

Cons:

When compared to other types of commercial property, apartment buildings are much more management intensive, and command far fewer dollars per tenant. In many cases, you would need to have forty residential tenants to command the same revenue as you would with four good commercial tenants, while having to keep up with ten times the landlord/tenant communication!

Furthermore, apartment buildings are generally single-purpose buildings, which limits you to residential tenants. Office, industrial and retail buildings are generally more favorably zoned, and can therefore be more easily rented to different types of tenants.

As I just mentioned, tenant rollover is higher with apartment buildings than it is with the other commercial property types. Apartment buildings often require an ongoing effort on the part of the landlord/manager in order to fill vacancies. Retail and industrial tenants, in particular, are far less likely to move because they are significantly more vested in their leaseholds. Add to this the fact that the standard residential lease is only one year, as compared to 2-5 years for industrial and office leases and 5-20 years with retail leases, and you can see why tenant rollover is a major consideration.

As compared to smaller residential properties, apartment buildings typically inspire less tenant loyalty, which results in a higher tenant rollover than you would have in a 2-4 plex.

Also, apartment buildings are ineligible for a residential loan, including FHA/VA financing options. These types of properties must be purchased with commercial loans, which are subject to higher interest rates and increased down payment requirements (as much as 30-40 percent). Furthermore, keep in mind that residential complexes with 5-6 units are notoriously difficult to finance as they are too large to qualify for residential financing, and too small to interest commercial lenders.

Another issue is that unlike 2-4 Plex residential properties, the value of an apartment building is based strictly on the rental income–and the rental income does not represent much of an upside when compared to that of other types of commercial real estate. A major facelift can dramatically increase the profitability of office and retail space, whereas cosmetic changes (while helpful and important) will only go so far with apartment buildings, which are often burdened with rent restrictions.

In my view, apartment buildings are not the best investment properties because they come with the downsides of commercial properties, but very few of the upsides.

After making my first million dollars, I purchased two apartment buildings in the city of Long Beach. My first apartment complex was a 9-unit building with a great unit mix, listed for $650,000. The second property I purchased was a 6-unit apartment complex.

I proceeded to renovate both of these apartment buildings with new carpet, interior painting and minor common area landscaping, and was able to increase the rents to market. After owning them for a year, however, I found out firsthand how management intensive they could be.

By that time the rental market was capping out, so I didn't see much more of an upside to holding on to these properties. I sold both at a significant profit and switched my focus to office properties, as office building prices were much lower than apartment building prices relative to the income the properties produced. I never looked back!

Office: Pros & Cons

Pros:

Office buildings are popular with real estate investors, which is always important when you go to sell the property down the line. When compared to apartment buildings or industrial or retail properties, I've always found office buildings to provide a heightened pride of ownership, and more of an opportunity to significantly increase the property's cosmetic appeal. Office buildings also provide the landlord with lots of potential for reducing operating expenses and thus increasing the property's net income and therefore its value. (As you will see in Play #9, making cosmetic improvements and reducing operating expenses are two key ways of increasing the value of your properties, so it is not insignificant that the office building provides the most opportunity to add value in these ways.)

Another great thing about office buildings is that as a landlord, you will be able to draw from a much broader tenant base than you would with retail and industrial properties. In an office building you can have tenants that are in the same business, whereas you would not want to mix competing retail tenants into the same center. In industrial properties it can be hard to find or replace tenants, both because the tenant base is smaller and because industrial tenants often have highly specialized needs. In a side-by-side comparison, it is definitely easiest to fill vacancies in office properties–which is good, because you are about to learn that a higher tenant rollover is among the downsides of investing in office buildings.

Cons:

One of the downsides to office buildings is that the landlord must contend with a higher tenant rollover as compared to retail or industrial properties, where the tenants generally have a much more vested interest in their space, and are therefore less likely to relocate. This is especially true during a recession, when you may find yourself competing with rapidly declining office rents in order to keep your tenants. (This particular downside can also work in your favor during recessions, when you can purchase office buildings very cheaply due to their reputation for high tenant rollover.)

Another downside to consider is that after apartment buildings, office buildings are the most management intensive of all commercial property types. Additionally, office buildings are usually full service, meaning the landlord is responsible for the costs of the utilities, insurance, and janitorial services, which translates to much higher operating expenses.

Industrial: Pros & Cons

Pros:

Of all the types of commercial real estate, industrial properties present the lowest risk to the investor. This is because industrial tenants, in general, are more stable than their office counterparts. Because of the nature of their work, they tend to have a more vested interest in the property. Compared to office tenants, it is much more difficult for industrial tenants to relocate. Even in a renter's market, industrial tenants are less likely to move.

Industrial properties are submetered for utilities, which are typically paid by the tenant. Another perk is that industrial leases are often net, double net or triple net leases. This means that beyond paying rent and utilities, the tenant pays some combination of insurance, maintenance costs, property taxes, and common area expenses, which are all expenses that are assigned to the landlord in most standard leases. (I use triple net leases with all of my industrial tenants, with very rare exceptions.)

Cons:

Industrial properties don't have the same curb appeal as retail centers or office buildings, especially the mid to high rise properties. They also don't appreciate as much. In addition, rental rates are lower, so the upside in terms of cash flow is less.

Industrial properties tend to be more management intensive than retail properties, but this downside is offset by the fact that the maintenance expenses are passed on to the tenants. Additionally, even though industrial tenants are extremely vested in their leasehold improvements and therefore less likely to move, it is worth noting that the average industrial lease is much shorter than the typical retail lease. The average industrial lease is 2-5 years, as compared to 5-20 years with retail.

Retail: Pros & Cons

Pros:

One of the upsides of retail buildings is that they serve a specific need in the community. This means that as long as a retail building is in a good location, occupancy is usually pretty consistent, which provides the landlord with a stable income.

Retail leases are usually long term (as mentioned above, the typical retail lease term ranges from 5-20 years) which also provides a certain amount of stability. Another upside to retail is that like industrial tenants, retail tenants are extremely vested in their leasehold improvements, making them more likely to renew their leases, again contributing to their stability as tenants.

Another perk is that like industrial properties, retail properties are separately metered for utilities. Finally, retail is the least management intensive of all commercial property types, and can offer significant curb appeal and pride of ownership.

Cons:

On the downside, the average 5-20 year lease term limits the financial upside for the investor in terms of rental revenues. Retail leases generally set rates for the long term, which limits the degree to which the landlord can make improvements and increase rents accordingly. Furthermore, the higher occupancy rates limit the potential for adding value by filling vacancies. Personally, I prefer office buildings over retail for this very reason.

Another major downside to consider is that the success of any retail center is very dependent upon the anchor tenant(s).

If the anchor tenant(s) falters or fails, the resulting loss of foot traffic creates a domino effect, and the smaller tenants in the building also suffer. This could then translate into tenant loss.

Also, compared to apartment buildings and even office properties, with retail properties it can take much longer to fill vacancies, due to the fact that you are often limited to tenants with the same type of business as the one that previously occupied the space. Filling retail vacancies is also tricky in the sense that you have to be careful not to bring in new tenants who would compete with your existing tenants too directly. For instance, if you already have one hair salon in a shopping center, another hair salon would not be the best new tenant to bring in to fill a vacancy.

Finally, as compared to office and industrial properties, there just aren't as many discounted retail properties to be found in the commercial market.

Final Thoughts

As you can see, each commercial property type has its ins and outs to consider as you weigh your options. At the very beginning of this play I was not shy about advocating for a shift to commercial properties. As I said, you will be able to grow the value of your portfolio much more quickly—and with far fewer deals—by shifting your focus to the commercial market. Once you decide to make this transition, keep in mind that while commercial deals are definitely more complex than residential deals, there is nothing you can't handle with your common sense, cojones, and a solid strategy.

In Play #7, I will give you the criteria to use when you buy commercial properties, so that you can find the properties that will make you the most money on the buy.

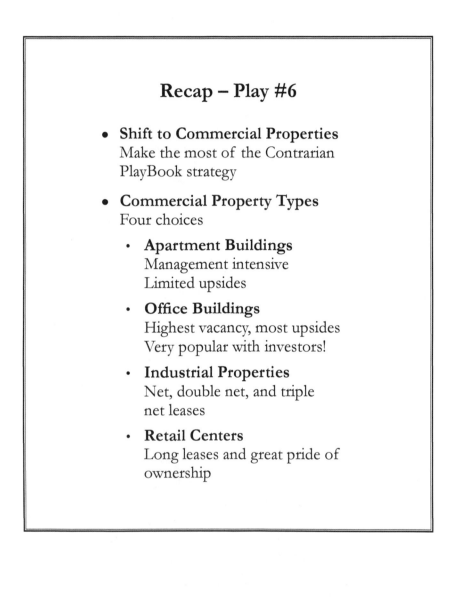

Recap – Play #6

- **Shift to Commercial Properties**
  Make the most of the Contrarian
  PlayBook strategy

- **Commercial Property Types**
  Four choices

  - **Apartment Buildings**
    Management intensive
    Limited upsides

  - **Office Buildings**
    Highest vacancy, most upsides
    Very popular with investors!

  - **Industrial Properties**
    Net, double net, and triple
    net leases

  - **Retail Centers**
    Long leases and great pride of
    ownership

Play #7

Pick A Winner: Commercial

The Winning Criteria

When picking a winning commercial property, the basic principles of the Contrarian PlayBook strategy apply: Since you want to make your money on the buy, you want to buy a discounted property—and since you want to sell at a high profit, you want to pick a winner! This is where your research and adherence to the Contrarian PlayBook's criteria will make all the difference.

In Play #6 you learned about the pros and cons of different commercial property types. The process of picking a winning commercial property will, in some areas, mirror the process of finding the right residential property.

As with residential properties, you begin by choosing a market and submarket that fit your overall objective. Then you will look for specific properties, using the criteria outlined in this play. Take the time to really understand each criterion, because each one is critical to making your money on the buy.

Define Your Market

A Metropolitan City

As with residential properties, you want to identify your market and submarket when beginning to look at commercial properties. When new to commercial investing, I still advise you to stay local, but if you do not live in a metropolitan area you will need to expand your definition of "local" to include the nearest metropolitan city. (For very experienced investors, Play #12 addresses the buying of properties even farther outside of your local area, but you will still want to study the criteria for commercial properties as presented in this play—they all hold true, regardless of where you are investing.)

In real estate, the term Metropolitan Statistical Area (MSA) refers to an urban area, and is determined by factors such as population and other community characteristics. Stick to investing in medium to large metropolitan cities, specifically those with good population growth and a low cost of living, because having a local economy that can sustain your investments is essential. Look for an MSA where the property values have already declined over 15 percent but are showing signs of stabilization.

Metropolitan cities are also more diversified, and present a much larger number of investment opportunities for you to consider. More properties on the market means more competition for sellers, which means more bargaining power for you—and more bargaining power for you means more money made on the buy!

Being well-located in a metropolitan city is also important when you are ready to sell. I have made the mistake in the past of buying in less metropolitan places, only to find that there wasn't enough movement in the local economy to attract enough buyers when it came time to sell, thus making these investments much less profitable.

Case in point: A few years back, I purchased a 6-story office building in Amarillo, Texas, which was anchored by Bank of America and the Gas Company. Even though the building had great curb appeal and income, Amarillo was such a small market that when it came time to sell, I had a bit of a struggle. There was not much activity, and therefore few comps were available. I ended up selling it for a profit, but it took me much longer than the other buildings I was selling at the same time in Houston.

Research Your Submarkets

When researching your commercial submarkets, remember that submarkets in a particular MSA can each be weathering the economy very differently. With commercial properties, you also want to pay particular attention to the issue of whether or not the property is sustainable by the local economy. Make sure that the submarket has an upside and is fluid—in other words, a submarket with enough listings so that you can buy at a discount, and enough demand so that when you sell, you will be able to do so at a profit.

So as you begin to look for commercial properties, you want to spend some time familiarizing yourself with a number of potential submarkets. Find the one that makes you the most money on the buy!

Criteria for Commercial Income Property

Criterion #1: Priced at a Discount

As with residential properties, a discounted sale price is at the very top of the criteria list and the very center of the Contrarian PlayBook strategy. It is the single most important aspect of making your money on the buy, and is an absolute must for any good investment property.

Remember that while foreclosures and other distressed properties account for a large percentage of discounted properties, you can find discounts in other sectors of the market as well—forgetting this could lead you to miss out on good opportunities.

A motivated seller can be a huge factor in securing a discounted sale price. In 1999, I bought my first shopping center from a man who had had two bypass surgeries, was retiring to Big Bear, and just wanted to get the property off his hands. His original asking price was $900,000, and it had been reduced to $700,000. Knowing the seller's situation, including the fact that he owned the property free and clear, I was able to negotiate a final price of $539,000.

When searching for a discounted property, stay focused on your objectives and find the property that will best help you to achieve your long-term goals. Common sense will tell you why this first criterion is central to a strategy that has you making your money on the buy, but in order for this strategy to be successful to the tune of $100 million, you need to pay attention to the following criteria as well.

Criterion #2: Priced Below Replacement Cost

This is the second most important criterion. The property is priced below replacement cost if the construction of a new and similar development in that area would cost more than the price you pay for your property. If you don't buy a property that is below replacement cost, you may very well find yourself competing with new construction coming to the area. By purchasing below replacement cost you have an advantage from the get-go, and will be able to be competitive with your rental/lease rates.

Failing to adhere to this criterion would cost you big if the building were ever to be rendered a total loss (by severe storm damage, for example), as insurance companies will only pay the building's replacement cost.

Replacement cost is based on material and labor costs, so it is constantly fluctuating. The best way to assess this is to ask an insurance agent, as they have metrics that they use specifically for calculating replacement costs.

Criterion #3: Potential for Adding Value

As with residential properties, you want to invest in commercial properties that have an upside—potential for adding value. Finding a value add property has two benefits: One, when you buy, you will have less competition from other buyers. Remember, as a contrarian you are among the few who will be going beyond first impressions and focusing on the building's potential. Two, when you sell, you will be able to do so at a greater profit because of the value you added.

There are three aspects to this criterion: Property Improvement, Occupancy, and Cash Flow.

Property Improvement:

The contrarian knows that the best investments don't have to look good! The contrarian looks for potential. This potential often lies in the physical condition of the building inside, and/ or the curb appeal outside–its cosmetic appeal. As with residential properties, instead of looking for cosmetic appeal, look for cosmetic appeal potential. If a property already looks great, you will find yourself competing with other buyers. On the other side of the spectrum, if a property isn't as pleasing to the eye, you may well be the only buyer who sees its potential, and your discounted price will be your prize. Furthermore, by buying a diamond in the rough, you will also be able to add value to the property by making cosmetic improvements, which will further increase your profits when you decide to sell.

Occupancy:

Apartment Buildings

When looking at apartment buildings, look for a building with a historical occupancy rate of around 70-80 percent. This is considered underperforming for these large residential properties and will factor into the discount you want to get–remember, you are making your money on the buy! Apartment buildings are generally considered "performing" at 90-100 percent occupied. Confirm that you've found an underperforming property by looking at the occupancy rates of other apartment buildings in the area.

Office Properties

When assessing a commercial property for value add potential, you will also need to look at the current occupancy level. The best buys are underperforming, and the ideal office property has an occupancy rate between 50 and 70 percent. This is the occupancy "sweet spot" and is a key factor in buying the right value add property.

An occupancy rate in this range probably means that the office property is poorly managed. It also typically means the property is stable enough to be a sound investment, while still leaving room to add value. In the context of making your money on the buy, these are good things: Now you can fix it up, lease it up, and increase the property's value in the process!

With this underperforming occupancy level, you can also increase your revenues by making the necessary improvements on the vacant units and renting them at higher prices than you would have been able to charge preexisting tenants.

Industrial Properties

For industrial properties, you will be looking for an occupancy rate of 60-70 percent. Again, always be focused on the goal of finding a building where you can add occupancy, and therefore value.

Retail Properties

When looking at retail properties, you generally want to find one that has an occupancy rate between 70 and 80 percent. With retail properties in particular, you need to keep in mind that what is considered to be "underperforming" varies from market to market. While 70-80 percent is considered underperforming in some areas, 90-95 percent would be considered underperforming in others. With this in mind, you will need to research the average occupancy rate for retail properties in your market. Personally, I don't invest much in retail because it doesn't offer as much of an upside in this regard.

Cash Flow:

Cash flow is the third aspect of this criterion. While positive cash flow is a good thing, in the Contrarian PlayBook strategy the best value add properties cash flow just above the break-even point. This leaves room for you to improve the cash flow (and therefore the value) of the property after you buy it. This will mean you want to find a property with a capitalization rate (cap rate) between 4 and 10 percent; this information can be found in the property listing.

The reason you want to stay on the positive side of the break-even point is that a positive cash flow will allow you to comfortably hold and lease a property until the market comes around and you are able to sell at a profit. Even in the event of a prolonged economic downturn, a property that cash flows will allow you to weather the storm without losing your shirt.

$$\textbf{Cap rate} \; = \; \frac{\textbf{Net Operating Income}}{\textbf{Sales Price}}$$

The cap rate is determined by dividing the NOI by the sales price. The Net Operating Income (NOI) is the net income after operating expenses. The capitalization rate (cap rate) projects the future income of the property and is used to estimate the value of an income-producing property. Appraisers will assign a cap rate to a property by considering the cap rates of recently sold similar properties in the area. The cap rate is a good measure of value as it relates to a property's income.

This is not to say that in order to be a profitable investment, a property has to cash flow. I have bought buildings with zero occupancy, and therefore zero cash flow. That said, properties that do not show cash flow at all are far riskier, and should only be considered if you are a very experienced investor.

Criterion #4: A Good Location

You've heard it before, and I'll say it again: Location, location, location! Just as with residential properties, location is something that cannot be changed, so you need to look at it right from the beginning of your search for a property.

In defining your market and submarkets for commercial properties, you already know you need to be focused on metropolitan cities. When it comes to the location of specific properties, you will look at issues of accessibility, crime, and noise—just as you did with residential properties.

Because of the residential nature of the apartment building, low crime is particularly important. Remember, a call to the local police station and an onsite visit can be invaluable when it comes to finding the right property.

When looking at location issues for office, industrial, and retail properties, you might be using a different measuring stick when looking at accessibility and noise (You will always want to find low crime locations). For instance, with commercial properties, a close freeway may be more of an asset than a problem. While office and retail tenants don't want an excess of traffic noise, they do want to be easily accessible, so noise could take a backseat to accessibility.

In addition, commercial tenants may look for other factors, such as proximity to local restaurants for their staffs, or the kind of visibility and/or foot traffic that will prosper their businesses.

Parking can be an important feature to offer both your tenants and your future buyers. In areas with lots of street parking or use of public transportation, the amount of on-site parking may not matter to the same degree. That said, parking is an amenity, and you want to be sure you measure up to the competition so you can attract—and keep—good tenants.

In general, if your future tenants would take these location issues into consideration, so should you.

Criterion #5: Diversified Tenant Base

A diversified tenant base is another important criterion. As a rule, I will not buy an office property in which any single tenant accounts for more than 20 percent of the building. In the retail and industrial markets, you want to avoid single-tenant properties, but the 20 percent rule does not hold true. With retail properties, a solid anchor tenant may account for more than 20 percent of the property occupancy, but in this case the anchor tenant is also bringing foot traffic to your other tenants, and so is considered a huge draw in attracting (and keeping) good tenants. With industrial properties, a credit tenant (a large regional or national, investment-grade tenant with excellent credit) will often account for more than 20 percent of the property, but this type of tenant is very low-risk. In addition, the resale value added to industrial property by a credit tenant is significant.

Single tenant properties are incredibly risky, as you are hanging your hat on the ongoing viability of a single entity. Things can change in any company, and with them the company's leasing needs. However attractive a single tenant building may look in every other way, a diversified tenant base is included in the criteria for good reason.

I have personally had Fortune 500 companies as tenants, and made the mistake of breaking the 20 percent rule on the assumption that these companies were established enough to be stable tenants. I learned the hard way that no company is immune to hard times.

I once bought a single tenant property in Dallas that was leased to CompUSA when their company appeared to be going strong. Six months later, they went bankrupt. I got bit again when I bought a building where Boeing was the single tenant. I bought it thinking that the government, who Boeing was contracted with, would be reliable–but when Boeing lost the contract, I ended up selling at a loss. I took a hit on these deals, but I learned my lesson. These are the only two properties that I ever sold at a loss, and both losses were because of single tenancy.

In addition to the tenant diversification, you will also need to consider the projected tenant rollover, which is the number of leases that are set to expire in a given time frame. Personally, I will not buy a property that projects more than 30 percent rollover in the first two years. Higher tenant rollover means higher risk, as well as having to spend more money on leasing costs in the near future.

Single tenancy or projected tenant rollover is not usually an issue with apartment buildings, but you will want to pay attention to a good unit mix. For more information on this, see the Additional Criteria for Apartment Buildings section after Criterion #6.

Criterion #6: Property Age

Lastly, I prefer to purchase buildings that were built after 1980. Buildings constructed before 1980 are more likely to have environmental issues, such as asbestos and lead contamination. Also, older buildings are often ADA non-compliant.

Additional Criteria for Apartment Buildings

There are two additional criteria to note about apartment buildings:

Criterion #1: Separately Metered for Utilities

This may well be the single most important criterion when it comes to apartment buildings. Not all apartment buildings are going to be separately metered for utilities. While almost all apartment buildings have one master water meter, it is critical that you only invest in those that are separately metered for electricity and gas.

This is not a minor issue. Some buildings are master metered for all utilities, meaning that you, as the landlord, are ultimately responsible for 100 percent of the utility costs – including those resulting from overusage or abuse of usage by your tenants.

Even though master metered properties are typically rented out at a higher rate per square foot to offset the utility costs, they still make for risky investments. If a tenant goes delinquent, for example, you will find yourself carrying a higher operational cost than you would with a separately metered building.

This is particularly important in states with extreme weather, which leads to increased usage of heat and/or air conditioning. In Arizona and Texas, for example, the operating costs for a master metered building can run almost 50 percent of the gross rents, largely due to high utility usage. This means that you would have to maintain a high occupancy to keep a positive cash flow, making it a risky investment.

Sticking to separately metered buildings will save you lots of landlord headaches and money, and will make it much easier to sell down the line. For all the reasons mentioned above, buyers prefer investing in properties with separately metered units—so don't stray from this criterion!

Criterion #2: Good Unit Mix

A good unit mix will make a big difference. The right apartment building should have some 3 bedroom units and at least 70 percent of the units should be 2 bedroom units. Remember, you are thinking about what kind of tenants you want and how much tenant rollover you will have to deal with—and unit mix makes a difference. A concentration of 2 bedroom units will also be a positive feature when you go to sell.

Find the Right Commercial Property

With commercial properties you will want to use a commercial MLS site, such as Loopnet or Costar. My Premier membership with Loopnet is well used! Finding and identifying the right discounted commercial property is key—use the criteria above as your guide.

To find out if the price is discounted, research the area in which you want to buy. Go online to search for whatever type of property you are looking for. Compare enough listings in that submarket to get a good grasp on what the average price is for similar properties. Specifically, you are going to be looking at the price per square foot and taking the time to arrive at a solid average, which will help you to more easily and accurately identify the discounted properties. From there, further focus your searches according to the remaining criteria.

Even if you are already a RE agent yourself, you might still want to reach out to local agents. Nothing like someone with an ear to the ground–that agent could be the secret weapon to your first million dollar profit in real estate!

Final Thoughts

I use these criteria on a constant basis. My portfolio hasn't "outgrown" them, and neither have I! They have served me well over the course of my career in real estate investment. Some of the criteria are common contrarian knowledge, and some I came to the hard way–through my mistakes along the way.

While I believe that each one of these criteria has a solid foundation in common sense, and that you can't go wrong by staying within their parameters, I would be less than honest if I said I never strayed from them myself. Sometimes, investing in a property that doesn't fit all the criteria has resulted in failure, such as the two single-tenant buildings I ended up selling at a loss. Other times, I have strayed from the criteria with deals that ended up being very profitable. This being said, the vast majority of the properties I buy fit all of the criteria discussed above. If your experience is anything like mine, you will find that you still have lots of flexibility in how you put together your $100 million real estate portfolio while operating within the guidelines of the criteria.

If you find yourself tempted to stray from the criteria, keep in mind that you will be taking an increased risk, however calculated, by doing so. With two decades worth of experience in real estate, I have developed a sixth sense when it comes to selecting property, as well as an ability to clearly see the big picture–but even now, on the rare occasions when I do deviate from the criteria, I know I am taking a heightened risk, and I make sure that I am operating within my risk tolerance.

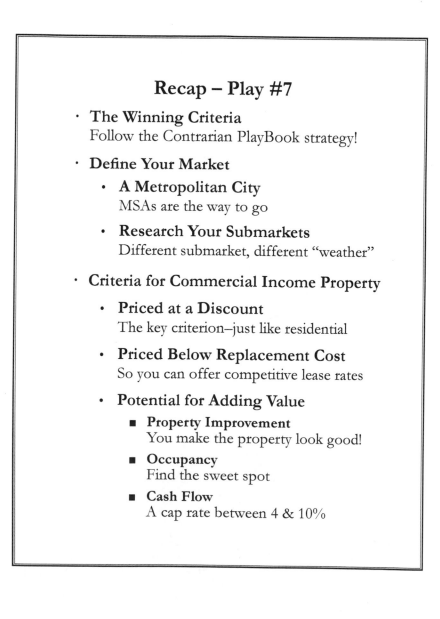

Recap – Play #7

- **The Winning Criteria**
  Follow the Contrarian PlayBook strategy!

- **Define Your Market**
  - **A Metropolitan City**
    MSAs are the way to go
  - **Research Your Submarkets**
    Different submarket, different "weather"

- **Criteria for Commercial Income Property**
  - **Priced at a Discount**
    The key criterion—just like residential
  - **Priced Below Replacement Cost**
    So you can offer competitive lease rates
  - **Potential for Adding Value**
    - **Property Improvement**
      You make the property look good!
    - **Occupancy**
      Find the sweet spot
    - **Cash Flow**
      A cap rate between 4 & 10%

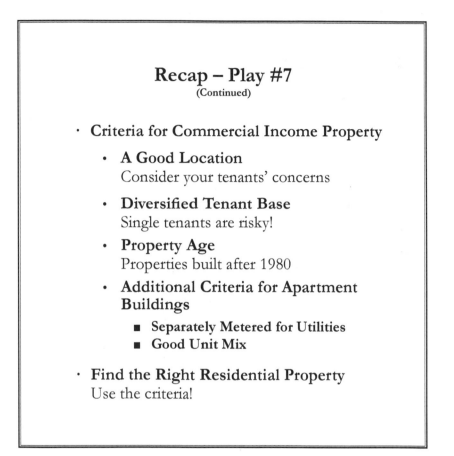

Recap – Play #7
(Continued)

· **Criteria for Commercial Income Property**

  · **A Good Location**
  Consider your tenants' concerns

  · **Diversified Tenant Base**
  Single tenants are risky!

  · **Property Age**
  Properties built after 1980

  · **Additional Criteria for Apartment Buildings**
    ▪ **Separately Metered for Utilities**
    ▪ **Good Unit Mix**

· **Find the Right Residential Property**
Use the criteria!

Play #8

Negotiate
From Strength

Making More Money on the Buy

Now that you have identified a property that you want to buy, the second aspect of actually making your money on the buy kicks in: Negotiation. Here your common sense will serve you well, as will the powerful strategy presented in this play. Follow it, and you will become the kind of negotiator who can build a $100 million portfolio, one successful deal after another.

Note: While some aspects of the negotiation strategy laid out in this play apply to all property types, there are some that apply only to commercial properties. In most cases, the difference is self-explanatory—where it isn't, I have provided clarification. No matter what type of property you are investing in, this play will help you make more money on your buy!

Your Strategy

Get Credible

Be a credible and serious buyer, and establish yourself as one. As I said in Play #2, this will facilitate every deal you ever make. Sellers are often inclined to choose a credible buyer with a lower offer over a buyer who offers more, but does not present with the same credibility.

When it comes to establishing your credibility, the more information you can provide upfront about your real estate experience the better. It will make you look steady and stable—in other words, someone they will be able to close escrow with. When you present yourself to the seller in this way, you are making it clear that this is not your first rodeo, and that you mean business. As a result, the seller (and the seller's agent) will see you as someone to be taken seriously.

In most real estate markets, but especially in the discounted property market, certainty of closing is the biggest and best thing you can bring to the negotiating table. Let them know from the get-go that you have both the interest and the means to make the sale happen. This will put you in a position of strength for the rest of the negotiation process.

Give to Get

Being willing to give in order to get is a key part of my investment strategy, especially as it applies to negotiation. Most sellers in the discounted property market are accustomed to potential buyers who, acting on the assumption that the seller is desperate, throw their weight around and make unreasonable demands.

On the other hand, if you demonstrate to the seller that you are willing to give in order to get, it will distinguish you from other buyers and inspire the seller to want to open escrow with you, and to meet your requests as you go through the various stages of negotiation.

This boils down to basic human psychology: A person who feels respected and considered is more likely to make concessions than a person who feels disrespected and bullied. This attitude works in the short-term, on any given deal, and in the long-term, where you develop a reputation as a real estate investor who is fair and reasonable, and gets deals closed.

Giving in order to get is in no way synonymous with weakness. In fact, the opposite is true: This style of negotiation puts you, the buyer, in a very favorable and strong position. Understand that this is not about giving everything away; it is about finding a balance that keeps a deal moving forward and, in the end, puts your name on the property's title.

The emotion that can easily trip you up here is greed, which might lead you to try and squeeze every last dollar out of a deal. Greed will make your life–and your seller's life–miserable, and can eat up a deal to the point of collapse. The irony is that by eliminating greed from your negotiations, and giving to get instead, it is highly likely that you will close a deal that, in the end, makes you more money on the buy!

First Contact: Call the Listing Agent

As you know, part of the process of picking a winning property involves looking at the property's listing history to determine how long it has been on the market, and what price reductions have been made. This step helps you to gauge the level of the seller's motivation to unload the property.

Now is the time for the next step, and this is one that requires some cojones: Pick up the phone and call the listing agent. There are two primary purposes to this initial phone call: One, to uncover basic information about the property that may not have been discernible from the research you have already done; and two, to get a better idea of the seller's level of motivation.

One of the first things I ask the agent is if there are any loans that can be assumed. Sometimes, an existing loan is a huge plus. If the existing loan has a much lower interest rate than the current market, great! For commercial properties, an existing loan may also benefit you if the balance is higher than 75 percent of the price you are willing to pay for the property, as this would allow you to come in with less than the traditional 25 percent down payment. In this scenario, you would be risking less money by assuming the existing loan. The potential downsides of assuming an existing loan would be if it has a higher interest rate, if it has a hefty prepay penalty, or if the loan matures in less than three years. If the existing loan has any of these downsides, you should obtain new financing.

Next, I ask the agent to confirm the current occupancy rate. I also ask if any of the tenants have recently vacated, and if there are any tenants in default of their lease agreement. For obvious reasons, you must assume that tenants defaulting on their lease agreements will negatively impact the property's financial projections moving forward. Finally, for commercial properties I also ask if there are any tenants who have gone dark, meaning they continue to pay, but do not occupy the space. This is particularly important for retail centers, as an empty space reduces foot traffic and makes the center look empty. In addition, tenants who have gone dark are not likely to renew their leases.

Finally, I ask the listing agent my favorite question: Is there any room for negotiation on the price? If so, how much? The listing agent will rarely give you an exact figure, but you will almost always be able to get a general idea. Remember, the agent is motivated to move the property as well, especially in a buyer's market—so if there is flexibility on the part of the seller, it is in the best interest of the agent to discuss this with you in your initial phone call.

If you get the sense that the seller doesn't want to budge, you would usually be better off setting your sights on another property. There are rare cases in which the listing price is so discounted that it would still be worth it to write an offer, even knowing that there may not be much room for further negotiation, but those cases are exceptions to the rule.

If the seller is motivated (which is most often the case in the discounted property market), schedule an appointment to see the property in person. If the walk-through doesn't raise any red flags, and the property appears to fit the criteria, you can get started on writing your initial offer.

First Round of Negotiations: The Offer

Writing The Initial Offer

Remember, making your money on the buy is not just about finding a discounted price on the listing; it is also about securing further discounts through negotiation, starting with the initial offer. Your initial offer sets the stage for the rest of the negotiation process.

Credibility

A good initial offer will hit hard, but since you do not want your offer dismissed, when you hit 'em hard, remember to also establish your credibility. Giving the seller the confidence that you are a serious buyer with the ability to close will nearly always get your foot in the door.

Provide documents that show your investment experience and your financial readiness. When I submit my letter of intent (LOI) with my initial offer on a property, I also send a pre-approval letter from my lender, a brief bio, a schedule of my real estate holdings (Buyer's Resume), references from brokers I have closed deals with, a current savings account statement and the first two pages of my most recent tax returns (with all confidential information blacked out, of course).

If you are not in a position to submit all of this information, just provide what you can. The idea is to speak to your strengths as a buyer. Try to at least submit a pre-approval letter from your lender, as this will go a long way towards setting yourself apart from the average buyer.

Incentives

While a good initial offer will hit hard, it will also include in-centives for the seller. There are three key ways in which you can incentivize the seller to accept your hard-hitting offer and move into escrow. The first is by offering to pay in cash—provided, of course, that you have the liquidity to do so, and that it fits your risk tolerance. Cash is king, especially in a down market. In my experience, offering all cash is 90 percent effective in securing a discount with the initial offer.

After my first million dollar deal, I bought an apartment complex. It was a 9-unit apartment building in the city of Long Beach, listed for $650,000. I made an all-cash offer of $550,000 with a $100,000 deposit and a 10 day escrow. I also purchased a 6-unit apartment building that was listed at $500,000 by making an offer of $400,000 cash with a 7 day closing. Cash is a great incentive!

The second way to sweeten the deal for the seller is to offer a shortened due diligence period. More than anything, the seller wants certainty of closing, and offering a shortened due diligence period sends the message that you are intent on making the deal happen quickly. From the seller's perspective, the shorter the escrow period, the less opportunity for you—the buyer—to change your mind about the property.

The third way you can incentivize the seller to accept your initial offer is by offering a sizable nonrefundable deposit. You can offer this after your short due diligence expires, or after you are certain your loan will be approved. Again, this indicates that you are serious about the property and that you fully intend to make the deal happen. A nonrefundable deposit is a layer of protection for the seller, and the fact that you are offering it up front demonstrates good faith on your part. This makes you a very attractive buyer.

What to Offer

There are a number of things to consider when calculating your initial offer, including the information you got from the listing agent. In addition to asking how much room there is in the asking price, I also ask what the seller would accept if I were able to close quickly, and whether or not they have received any full price offers.

To a certain extent, you can also base the amount of your initial offer on what incentives you can provide to the seller. If you can offer all of the above mentioned incentives, you are in the best position to have your offer accepted, even over a competing offer that may be higher, but does not incentivize the seller.

One morning I received a "grab your checkbook" call. It was for a beautiful bank-owned house valued at $9.2 million. It had been listed by the bank at $8 million, before eventually being dropped to $5,999,900. As I mentioned earlier, there are rare cases in which the listing price is so discounted that you can buy it without negotiating further price reductions, and this was one of those rare finds. I made an offer of $6 million ($100 over the asking price!) with $250,000 down as a nonrefundable deposit and a three-week closing. The bank had another offer that was much higher than mine, but it also had a 45 day contingency and a 30 day closing. Banks are not in the business of managing real estate, and they typically want foreclosures off their books as soon as possible—so my offer was accepted.

Even though this deal was atypical, I share it with you here because it so perfectly illustrates that when all is said and done, the most valuable thing you can offer a seller is certainty of closing. In this particular deal, I offered the seller all three of the incentives we just reviewed.

If you do not have the liquidity to offer either all cash or a substantial and nonrefundable deposit, don't get discouraged. If you are ready to go with a lender-approved loan application for the property, you will still have the ability to offer the seller a shortened escrow and due diligence period, which is often the greatest incentive of all.

Once you have calculated your initial offer, draft your LOI. The primary purpose of the LOI is to communicate your intentions to the seller, which you will do in the first few lines. Next you will detail the terms and conditions of your offer. Near the end you should include a clause that designates the document as non-legally binding. It is important to present yourself in a professional light in this letter. The LOI, and anything else you send with it, will form the seller's first impression of you—so make it a good one!

Initial Offer Checklist

- Write your Letter of Intent
  - Include incentives for the seller

    Cash

    Short escrow/due diligence period

    Nonrefundable deposit

- Compile relevant documentation to boost your credibility, including:
  - Pre-approval letter from your lender
  - Brief bio
  - Schedule of real estate holdings (Buyer's Resume)

- References from brokers you have closed deals with
- A current savings account statement
- First two pages of your most recent tax returns

Counter Offers

Once you've submitted your offer, follow up to confirm that the seller has received it, and ask when you can expect a response. Typically, you can expect to hear back from the seller within three business days.

If the seller submits a counter offer, try to get feedback from the seller's agent regarding what the seller is looking for. Sometimes the seller wants a shorter closing, or is already working with a set bottom-line sale price. Listen closely to what the agent tells you—sometimes the response will be very direct, but you may occasionally have to read between the lines. In any case, listen so that you can deliver. Give to get, and get the deal done!

It is worth noting that in real estate investment, you may have to write offers on a number of properties before you have one accepted. Sometimes there are factors beyond your control, no matter how much you want to make a deal happen. I write lots of offers, and therefore when some fall through or are rejected, it doesn't slow down my portfolio development. When I bought my first two apartment buildings in Long Beach, I made over thirty-five offers before those two were accepted! This is an extreme example, but illustrates the importance of casting a broad net when it comes to writing offers.

Accepted Offer

Once a seller does accept your offer, you will be provided with a contract, which should be reviewed by your real estate attorney. As I said in Play #3, a real estate attorney is not required for smaller residential deals, as you can rely on the title company to alert you of any red flags during escrow, such as substandard or contractor liens. For larger commercial deals, however, a good real estate attorney will be an important member of your team. Once the contract is fully executed, celebrate! You are officially in escrow.

Second Round of Negotiations: Escrow and Due Diligence

Escrow (and your due diligence period) begins when escrow receives your initial deposit along with your fully executed contract. The three key components of due diligence are property inspections (including ALTA surveys and other reports), tenant interviews, and the collection and analysis of the seller's current financials.

It is critical to be thorough when doing your due diligence, as the information you uncover will bring to light any potential problems with the property. In some cases, these problems are serious enough to be considered deal breakers. In other cases, they can provide the basis for any additional price reductions you request from this point forward.

Property Inspection

The first phase of due diligence is property inspection. Immediately after the contract execution, and prior to the formal property inspections, you will need to request the following documents pertaining to the property's condition:

Property Inspection Checklist

- Environmental Site Assessment reports (ESAs, Phase I and II if any)

  A Phase I ESA involves a preliminary assessment of the land and building. The assessor analyzes the property, including property records, for any heightened potential for hazardous substance contamination (i.e. gasoline from nearby gas station tanks or chemicals from dry cleaner sites). If the current mortgage holder hasn't already had a Phase I ESA performed, you will need to do so.

  If the Phase I ESA suggests possible contamination, a Phase II ESA is performed. Phase II ESA uses chemical analysis to determine the extent of the suspected contamination.

- ALTA Survey

  The ALTA survey will show the property lines, and reveal if there are any encroachments/ easements that would affect the property, as well as showing the locations of major building improvements.

- Property Condition reports (if any)

  This is intended to be a full disclosure report from the seller, noting any known problems with the property, or anything else that would generally be considered material to the transaction.

- Certificate of Occupancy

    This document is typically issued by the local building department, and confirms that the building is in compliance with relevant building codes and that it is fit for occupancy.

- Title report

    The title report is prepared once escrow opens, and shows the buyer how the title is currently held. Also noted in the report are any liens, easements, or encumbrances to the title that might affect ownership.

Having gathered the relevant documents, the next step is to schedule your inspection. An experienced property inspector is an invaluable member of your team. The inspector will examine the property for code violations, such as ADA, fire and safety. This will potentially include code issues that were previously grandfathered in but will need to be fixed moving forward. The inspector should be able to tell you the number of years remaining on the roof and give you a status report on the heating and cooling systems, as well as the condition of the plumbing, electrical wiring, foundation, and other key structural elements. In addition, make sure your inspector looks for asbestos and mold, which are both considered health hazards and can be expensive to address. If your inspector recommends a specialist to deal with the asbestos or mold, make sure to follow through on the recommendation.

I cannot stress enough the value of performing thorough inspections on the property. On almost every deal, I have problems brought to my attention as a result of the inspections. These problems range from code and safety issues to small problems with the roof or AC, and each one contributes to what is known as deferred maintenance/capital improvements.

As the deferred maintenance issues rise, you, the buyer, have increasing leverage to negotiate further discounts. In particular, safety issues uncovered by the inspections will be key to your negotiations. In order to arrive at the deferred maintenance costs, you will need to get contractor estimates for the work that needs to be done on the property. When you submit your revised offer, the inspection report and contractor estimates will be included.

Tenant Interviews

The second major component of due diligence is the performance of tenant interviews. By this point, you know that the property fits the tenant occupancy and tenant rollover criteria. Interviewing the tenants will provide you with the opportunity to confirm the projected tenant rollover and potentially uncover building issues that the inspections may not have identified.

Tenant Interview Checklist*

1. How do you like leasing at this building?
2. Are there any issues that you would like to discuss?
3. If and when we close escrow, is there anything we can do to improve your stay here?
4. How is business?
5. Would you say your company's finances are improving?

6. Are your company's finances weaker or stabilized over the past two years?

7. When your lease expires in _____, will you be renewing?

*Questions 4-6 apply to commercial properties only

Don't expect to be able to interview every tenant; for commercial properties you should focus on interviewing the major tenants, the ones that comprise the largest percentages of the property's rent/lease revenues. Also prioritize interviews with tenants who are coming up for renewal in the next six months. In addition to any property issues (such as elevator problems or a disruptive tenant in the building) that you might discover in these interviews, you will be looking for anything that is at odds with what you know to be the projected tenant rollover. If you find out that a tenant is going to be leaving, you can back that rent out and annualize it, then use it to negotiate a lower price.

Current Financials (for Income Properties)

The third phase of due diligence is analyzing the property's current financial documentation. Most real estate listings will list pro forma financial information, based on the assumption of a continual increase in profits. It is absolutely essential to gather the necessary financial documents in order to verify the actual income against the pro forma numbers on the listing. This, obviously, does not apply to condos and SFRs.

On the next page, there is a due diligence checklist of the financial information I request from the seller of a commercial property during escrow.

Financial Document Checklist

- P&L statements for the last 3 years, and year to date (YTD)
- Copies of current leases
- Pending new leases and renewals schedule
- Most recent certified rent rolls
- All vendor contracts
- Aged receivables
- Capital expenditure list
- Property tax assessments and bills, last 3 years and current
- 5-year insurance loss history reports

While you can request financial documents from the seller prior to escrow, the seller is under no obligation (and would have little motivation) to share this information with you until you are both under contract. Typically, you can expect to receive current financials from the seller between five and ten days after you open escrow.

Once you receive the current financials, there are very basic formulas you can use to analyze the information in order to more accurately calculate the income.

First, you would take the P & L statements and go through all of the expenses they have listed, checking for any items they may have backed out or that may change moving forward. For example, if the management fees are not listed because the current landlord self-manages, and you plan to hire a management company, you will need to factor that in (usually 2.5-4 percent of the gross rents per year.) Something else to look for could be an unrealistically low insurance premium, which could happen if the landlord has underinsured the building. This analysis will give you a more accurate practical expense figure.

Cap Rate and Cash on Cash Return

Once you have come up with a practical expense figure, you look at the revenue. Use the most recent rent roll to arrive at an accurate number for the annual gross income, then subtract the annual practical expenses to arrive at the net operating income (NOI). As you learned in Play #7, you will then divide the NOI by the sales price in order to arrive at an actual cap rate. The cap rate indicates what your rate of return would be on this property, given the practical/market expenses and assuming you paid all cash.

Of course, if you are obtaining third party financing for the purchase, you will need to include your mortgage payments in the practical expense figure to determine your Before-Tax Cash Flow (BTCF), which is your NOI less the debt service on your mortgage. Use this to determine your cash on cash return.

$$\textbf{Cash on Cash Return} = \frac{\textbf{BTCF}}{\textbf{Cash Invested}} \times 100 = \_\_\_\%$$

Keep in mind that you will always have other costs that are not considered part of your operating expenses, such as leasing commissions, tenant improvements, and capital improvements, which are all usually amortized over a period of years but directly affect your cash flow. You should consult your tax advisor on these expenses. In order to better analyze your cash flow, you will need to use estimated amortized expenses for these items so that you can arrive at a more solid cash flow number and see if this investment works for you. This is where the property condition assessments and contractor estimates come in handy, as they help you to more accurately project the costs of capital improvements that need to be made.

Another thing to analyze in terms of expenses would be the rent roll. You will need to note how many tenants are coming up for renewal, as tenant leases will typically cost you to renew, especially in a tenants' market. Typically, lease renewals on office buildings will cost you 3 percent commission for the entire term of the lease (as opposed to residential lease renewals, which normally cost nothing).

When renewing a lease or negotiating a new lease with a new tenant, you will also usually need to factor in an allowance for tenant improvements (TI), which are improvements made to the space by the landlord in order to accommodate the needs of the tenant. Because my investment strategy involves existing buildings vs. new construction, TI are normally restricted to new carpet and paint, so I budget about $2 per square foot for lease renewals, and $10 per square foot for new leases. (Note: While I budget $10 per square foot for TI on most commercial properties, for retail spaces I budget $20 per square foot.)

Potential NOI

Now that you've arrived at a reasonable understanding of the property's cash flow, and calculated realistic projections of the cash flow moving forward, the next step is to calculate the property's potential NOI. In order to do this, you first arrive at the average rental rate per foot by dividing the occupied square footage by the rent roll. Next, you take the average rental rate per foot and multiply it by the remaining (unoccupied) square footage, which when added to the current rent roll will show how much you would be making if the building were 100 percent occupied. Then, knock 10 percent off this figure in order to arrive at the gross revenue based on a 90 percent occupancy rate, which is a more realistic number to project. Adjust the rent per foot to market rate, if the current rate is below market.

Now you have the information upon which you will base your assumptions for the property. By subtracting your practical operating expenses from the gross revenue at 90 percent occupancy and market rate, you arrive at the potential NOI, also referred to as pro forma numbers. The potential NOI projects the increase in revenues that you can reasonably expect in the future. Make sure that when calculating the potential NOI for office buildings, you also factor in the increase in utilities and janitorial expenses that comes with increased occupancy.

Potential Sales Price

The last step is to take the pro forma numbers and divide them into the current market cap rate. This gives you the potential sales price you can expect for this asset if you stabilize it at, for example, 90 percent occupancy. (Keep in mind that different cap rates are used depending on the type of construction. Class A buildings with newer construction would be analyzed using a lower cap rate than older, class B buildings, but for most discounted properties you would use an 8-10 percent cap rate.)

Once you've made all of the above calculations, you will typically find that there was a certain amount of fluffing and/ or speculation that went into the pro forma financials on the listing. Any loss of income that you can calculate from the current financials can be used as a basis for further price reduction. For example, if you calculate a decrease in income of $50,000 per year, and project that forward at an 8 percent cap rate, this forms the basis for a request for a $400,000 price reduction. Even if you don't get the price reduction you ask for, you can make the case for some sort of concession from the seller.

Based on all of these calculations, you will now know for sure if you have found a diamond in the rough. The next step is to take all of your findings from the various aspects of the due diligence process, and use them to calculate your revised offer.

The Revised Offer

Now that you have performed the inspections and tenant interviews and have gathered and analyzed the current financials, it is time to write your revised offer.

Occasionally, due diligence won't provide you with much upon which to base a request for an additional price reduction. This is rare, but it happens—every deal is different! In cases like these you can go ahead with the purchase, because you've already made money on the buy twice: Once from the discounted listing price, and once from your initial offer and counter offer negotiations. Furthermore, since the property fit all of your criteria, there is still plenty of opportunity for you to increase the value of the asset once you own it.

Assuming that due diligence did provide you with reasons to request an additional price reduction, the next step is to compile your inspection report, contractor estimates, relevant tenant interview information and revised financial projections, and submit them with a cover letter detailing your revised offer. Make your presentation professional and clear. Be prepared to offer an additional nonrefundable deposit in exchange for the price reduction. Give in order to get, but balance it with remembering that these issues–especially the code and safety issues–will be on your doorstep once the contract goes through.

On a recent purchase of an office building, I had contractor estimates that added up to $638,000. In the interest of closing the deal, I submitted these estimates to the seller and suggested we meet halfway, saying I would settle for a $320,000 price reduction. The seller countered with an offer of a $250,000 price reduction, which I accepted.

As this deal illustrates, I offered to meet the seller halfway, and still agreed to his counter offer. In drafting your revised offer, you must remember to be reasonable with the seller. Keep in mind that you both have the same objective, which is to close the deal and close it quickly.

Note that because I had already negotiated substantial discounts on this already discounted property, I did not have to make totalitarian demands. Instead, I could afford to meet the seller in the middle.

As important as it is not to get greedy, it is equally important not to give in to fear–after all, you are a contrarian. By this stage of escrow, most buyers would be very emotionally invested in the idea of owning this property, and the fear of the deal falling apart could get in the way of asking for an additional price reduction, especially one of any significance. Remember, you have nothing to lose: You are already in escrow with a motivated seller, and the price reduction you are requesting is based on well-founded, well-documented information. Deferred maintenance costs and subsequent price reductions are expected in the discounted property market, and are a natural byproduct of the due diligence process, so your request will not come as a shock to anyone.

At this point, you can sweeten the deal for the seller by removing any remaining contingencies, which will make the seller that much more amenable to meeting your requests. This is another way in which you can stand out as a buyer: The typical investor wants it all, the discounts and the contingencies, through the last day of closing. In addition, you will be well prepared and so may be able to bump up the closing date. That is always a great card to be able to play. Give to get, and get the deal done!

The Final Inspection

The last step before closing is the final inspection. This is important, because anything can happen in real estate! A tenant could go dark overnight, or someone could crash into a garage door causing structural damage. It is essential to perform a thorough final inspection on the property right before closing to make sure nothing significant has changed from the time you first entered into escrow. If you do find anything irregular in your final inspection, you will need to decide whether it is significant enough to justify writing another revision to your contract.

Closing

You officially close on a property by wiring your payment to the escrow account. The title company will then record the deed. Before you do so, there are a number of things you will need to do. You will need to check for the correct prorationing of rents, security deposits, and property taxes on your estimated closing statement before you close; any adjustments will have to be made before you transfer funds. You will also want to arrange for pick-up of the original leases, as well as all property files and keys.

It's also prudent to obtain estoppel certificates from every tenant. Estoppel certificates confirm the amount of deposit on hand with the seller, as well as detailing rental payments and any outstanding issues the tenants may have with the seller. This is a common request in commercial real estate deals, and one that many lenders require. (Make sure to request the certificates two weeks prior to closing.)

You will also need to transfer all utilities, and notify your tenants of the change of ownership. Finally, don't forget to tell your new tenants where to send their rent!

No matter how many times you close on a property, it is always a great feeling! Each deal you close will earn you that much more credibility as an investor, and bring you that much closer to your $100 million real estate portfolio.

Final Thoughts

If you implement the Contrarian PlayBook strategy, negotiation can be the most exciting part of a real estate transaction. Ultimately, your negotiation skills are going to be what make–or break–every deal you are involved in. Knowing how to pick a winning property is one thing–securing it at a price that makes you money on the buy is another thing entirely, and is a critical part of being truly successful in real estate investment.

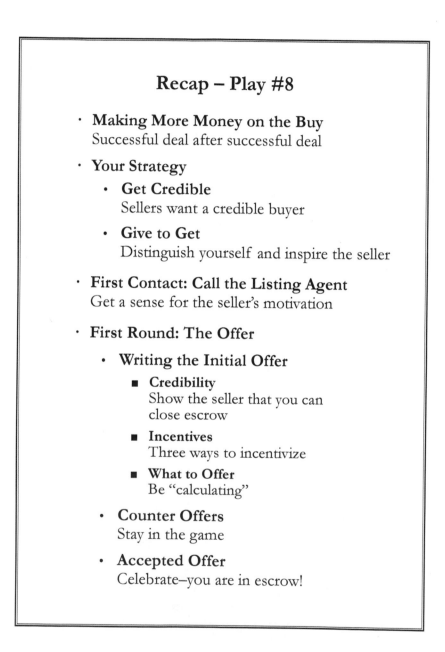

Recap – Play #8

- **Making More Money on the Buy**
Successful deal after successful deal

- **Your Strategy**
  - **Get Credible**
  Sellers want a credible buyer

  - **Give to Get**
  Distinguish yourself and inspire the seller

- **First Contact: Call the Listing Agent**
Get a sense for the seller's motivation

- **First Round: The Offer**

  - **Writing the Initial Offer**
    - **Credibility**
    Show the seller that you can close escrow

    - **Incentives**
    Three ways to incentivize

    - **What to Offer**
    Be "calculating"

  - **Counter Offers**
  Stay in the game

  - **Accepted Offer**
  Celebrate—you are in escrow!

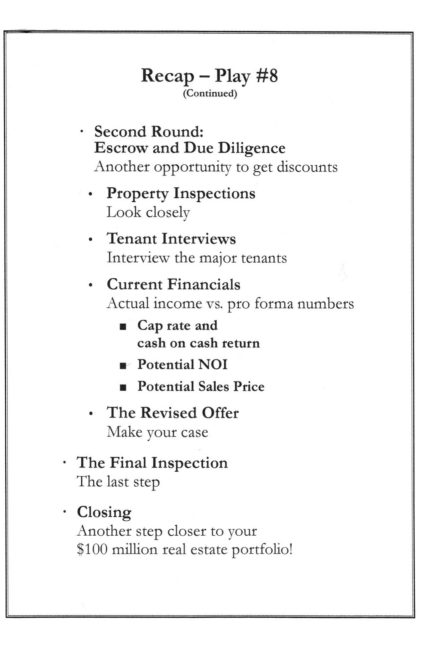

Recap – Play #8
(Continued)

- **Second Round:
  Escrow and Due Diligence**
  Another opportunity to get discounts

  - **Property Inspections**
    Look closely

  - **Tenant Interviews**
    Interview the major tenants

  - **Current Financials**
    Actual income vs. pro forma numbers

    - **Cap rate and
      cash on cash return**
    - **Potential NOI**
    - **Potential Sales Price**

  - **The Revised Offer**
    Make your case

- **The Final Inspection**
  The last step

- **Closing**
  Another step closer to your
  $100 million real estate portfolio!

STAY IN
THE GAME

LIVE IT!

When it comes to real estate investing, I love it all. I love the big picture and the small details. I love using my common sense to transform discounted properties into profits, often by turning distressed buildings into gems. It feels like magic–and that is a powerful feeling!

I also love playing like a contrarian. Being the guy outside the box and ahead of the curve never gets old! Living like a contrarian makes my whole life more interesting–and more fun. Combining commitment, common sense, and cojones–the three C's–is a great formula for a dream life.

Real estate investing has changed my life. In fact, I can't even believe the life I have today. I am married to a beautiful woman I truly love, my family and friends are behind me all the way, and I am lucky enough to be able to share my prosperity with my loved ones.

They say that when you love what you do, you never work a day in your life. I went through some very hard times before I found real estate investment, and I certainly put in a lot of days that truly felt like work. But all of that hard work paid off, and got me to where I am today.

Believe in Yourself

When I immigrated to this country with my family, we faced many challenges. I felt like I was in a jungle, fighting my way through each day. Not speaking the language made everything harder. For two years, I dedicated three hours a day to learning English, which required me to set my own drive and believe in myself. It was no easy task, but I made the investment of time and work because I knew I was worthy of that investment.

151

Be Persistent

Of the many lessons my father has taught me, one of the greatest is that persistence wears down resistance, and is an important part of any game plan. When our family was living in the car and my father had no job, he simply went out every single day and looked for one. Through all the hardship, he persisted with consistent action.

If you were to graph your persistence you would not want it to look like the graphs of economic cycles, up and down. Instead, you would want to see a steady, unfaltering line. Inevitably, life has its own ups and downs—but by maintaining a persistent commitment to your goals, you will be able to overcome any challenges you face along the way.

Don't Be Afraid of Failing

Thomas Edison said "Genius is 1 percent inspiration and 99 percent perspiration." This is because he knew failure. He is said to have failed 1,000 times on his way to his successful light bulb, but he apparently saw each attempt as a lesson in how not to make a light bulb.

My failures have been some of my best lessons. When you hit the down times in business, it is very easy to give up and stop taking action—but that is exactly when action is most needed! As a high school senior, I started my own business selling dried fruits and nuts door-to-door. I had been the top salesman for a multi-level marketing company selling the same items, but when I saw the prices at Price Club, I figured I could do it myself, at a greater profit. I quickly grew to five employees and was making about $4,000 a month. Since I did not realize all the regulations around selling food items, I eventually got shut down by the health department. Live and learn! Luckily, it did not shut down my entrepreneurial spirit.

Keep Learning

Remember that if you want to stay ahead of the curve and in front of the pack, you will need to continue to keep learning, and a learning mind is an open mind. Having an open mind will help you to successfully adapt to changing circumstances, which will definitely serve you in your real estate investment career. In my view, it is the constantly changing landscape of real estate investment that makes it so much fun.

An open mind is also willing to change. Before I got into real estate, I had two supermarkets, which were work-heavy seven days a week–the kind of work that felt like work. At one point, they were quite successful, but the toll on me was huge. Even if you own your own business, everyone is ultimately paid hourly. It felt like my hourly wage was far below what I had envisioned, and I did not feel like I was truly headed to my financial freedom–but because I was willing to change, I was able to take the big leap to real estate. I have never looked back!

Don't Be Afraid to Ask

Asking is an action as powerful as any. In the early 90's, I met a guy with a nice Porsche, and did not hesitate to ask him how he got to be so successful. It turned out he owned a mortgage company. I then asked him if he needed help, and he gave me a job!

I never stopped asking questions, about how loan process worked, or how he started his business. I was like a sponge, just absorbing all that I could learn. Because I was not afraid to ask questions, I ended up with a job and a real estate license, and unbeknownst to me, the real estate license would end up being more important than I ever could have imagined.

Stay Active

Staying in the game is key. I have turned every rejection I have faced, personally and professionally, into motivation to succeed. I have turned every setback and challenge into the commitment to move forward. Through the most personal places of rejection and prejudice to the collapses of business ventures, I have stayed in the game, and I have stayed in to win, not just survive.

Action is by nature rooted in the here and now. Action planned for the future or already accomplished is not action, because it is not now! Taking action will show you what works, and what doesn't. Take what works and create your success. Understand that this is a game you can win. Game on!

Let's Gooooo!

Play #9

Add Value
To Your Properties

The Value of Potential

Thanks to the limited number of contrarians out there, a good-looking property that shows a steady profit is always going to be more salable than a property that needs a little work, regardless of the state of the economy. While the average real estate investor is drawn to the beautiful, well-kept property with high occupancy and an impressive built-in revenue stream, the contrarian knows that the real value of a property lies in what it could be. It is through the process of bringing a property to its full potential that the contrarian adds value, which translates into a big payday when it comes time to sell.

As we saw in Play #7, the contrarian seeks out properties with an "upside"–those that are underperforming in terms of occupancy levels, cash flow, and appearance, inside and out. Not coincidentally, these criteria correspond to the three keys ways in which you can add value to your properties.

- Value Add #1: Make Cosmetic Improvements

  The right property has major potential for cosmetic improvement, giving you the opportunity to add value by making positive changes to the building and grounds.

- Value Add #2: Lease Up (Fill Vacancies)

  The right property has underperforming occupancy, so that you can create value by leasing out the vacant units and increasing revenue.

- Value Add #3: Reduce Operating Expenses

  The right property has cash flow, but ideally just enough to sustain itself. This is so that you can add value by cutting expenses and making operations more efficient.

You can (and should) get started with the process of adding value to your property as soon as you close escrow. The faster you can implement these improvements, the sooner you will have your property ready to sell–and the more prepared you will be to act fast and sell high when the market presents you with the opportunity. Even if you buy during a prolonged recession and end up holding on to the property for several years until the market turns, you will still benefit from making these improvements as quickly as possible. The more cash flow you are able to establish early on, the better equipped you will be to comfortably wait out even a long economic downturn.

Value Add #1: Make Cosmetic Improvements

The contrarian knows that the way to secure the best ROI in real estate is to buy the property that nobody wants, and transform it into the property that everybody wants. The first step in this transformation is making cosmetic improvements.

As soon as I close escrow on a property, I start moving on making necessary cosmetic improvements to the interior, exterior, and landscaping. Based on the surrounding buildings– the competition–and my budget, I prioritize what cosmetic improvements to make. Not all of these improvements are costly; you would be amazed at what can be done with a deep cleaning. I have all of my properties power washed, which makes a huge difference! To me it's just common sense, like washing your car before you sell it. Deep cleaning the interior and exterior will clearly reveal what your priorities should be in tackling more involved cosmetic changes, such as painting and recarpeting.

When it comes to these more involved changes, your immediate focus should be on the vacant units. In the first 90 days after closing escrow on a new property, I send my team in to "standardize the vacancies," which involves painting all the walls the same color, removing the existing carpet (assuming it needs replacing, which is almost always the case with discounted properties), deep cleaning the floor, and recarpeting if necessary. More detail-oriented changes such as standardizing the light fixtures, switch/outlet covers and door hardware are subtle changes that go a long way in improving your property's appearance.

It is generally safe to assume that any cosmetic changes you make will pay for themselves many times over. In terms of improvements to a property, cosmetic improvements generally offer the greatest ROI.

In 2005 I purchased a twelve story building in Houston for $12.5 million. I modernized it by painting the outside black, which cost $45,000. I installed mirrors in the elevator lobbies on each floor for a total of $30,000. I also fixed up the lobby and made some other minor cosmetic improvements. To top it off, I hung a huge Khoshbin flag outside: Talk about pride of ownership! All told, I spent around $100,000 on cosmetic changes, and turned it around at a $5 million profit, selling it for $17.5 million two years later. In this case the value added was almost entirely in the form of cosmetic improvements, as I did very little in terms of leasing up or cutting expenses. By improving the property's appearance, I increased the value by 40 percent! Never underestimate the power of curb appeal.

Making cosmetic improvements serves multiple purposes. When you come in as the new owner and make these improvements right off the bat, it boosts the morale of the existing tenants, and shows them that you are a hands-on owner who is taking an active interest in the property, which in turn makes them more likely to want to stay on when their leases expire. When it comes time to sell, the cosmetic improvements you've made will help you move the property faster and at a higher price, because the building will look good—which, after all, is what looks good to most buyers! In the interim, it will make it infinitely easier to lease the vacant units, which brings us to the second way to add value to your property: Leasing Up.

Value Add #2: Lease Up (Fill Vacancies)

Once you've made your cosmetic improvements, your next focus will be leasing the vacant units. The increased revenues will sustain you through even a prolonged economic downturn, giving you the freedom to comfortably hold the property until you can sell high.

There are several ways to attract prospective tenants. One way to do this is by advertising in the local newspaper. You can also post on Loopnet and Costar. Don't forget to reach out to the local community and let them know that the building is under new ownership. Since you bought a highly discounted asset, it's very likely that it has a less than golden reputation. Your goal is to attract local businesspeople who may have never considered leasing space in that building.

Another way to attract prospective tenants is to incentivize them. I like to hang a 30-foot "Under New Ownership" banner on the exterior of the building, advertising special introductory lease rates (i.e. "Sign a 3 Year Lease Now, and Get 6 Months Free Rent!"). Another way to advertise these special rates is to mail fliers to surrounding buildings. I do this with all of my properties, because in my experience it is an extremely effective way of leasing up quickly.

Just as making your money on the buy makes it possible for you to give to get in the negotiation process, so does it allow you to incentivize new tenants to lease from you. Since you bought the property at such a discounted rate, and because it was (at the very least) breaking even with its existing occupancy, you can afford to offer leases at below market rates to get new tenants in the door. I will often go so far as to advertise leases at half the going market rate for the first year. I then bump the rates a bit the second year, and a bit more the third year, but I'm still able to keep them under market value, which gives me a competitive edge in a tenant's market. You have to be competitive if you want to fill up those vacancies, and you want to fill up those vacancies as soon as possible, both for cash flow purposes and to make it more attractive to future buyers. Remember, most buyers want performing, not underperforming!

On the other hand, keep in mind that if the rates are too low, you may have a harder time selling it. In most cases where I do a lot of leasing up, I don't intend to sell right away. Usually, I aim to sell these properties in the second or third year. By the time I'm ready to sell the lease rates are closer to the market rate, but still competitive.

Another way to get tenants in the door is by advertising on-site management, on your banner and in any print advertising you do. Prospective tenants are more likely to spontaneously check out your property if they know that there is someone physically in the building who can answer their questions. We will further discuss the benefits and logistics of onsite management in Play #10, but for the purposes of this play it is sufficient to say that it will make your property more attractive to prospective tenants.

Yet another way to attract new tenants is to add amenities to the building. I frequently designate a room in my office buildings as a conference room to be shared between the tenants. Each tenant is given a key to the conference room, and they book it through the onsite management. In other cases, I have put in other amenities, such as a deli or an exercise room. Occasionally, a building will have what is known as a dead space, such as a basement, which can be turned into a functional space, such as a storage area, with minimal remodeling. Rent the storage to your tenants for a couple hundred dollars a month—now it's not only an amenity for your tenants, but an added source of income for you!

Think outside of the box for ways that you can compete with other area landlords, and lease up those vacancies! By filling up the vacant units, you will be transforming an under performing property with break-even books into a stabilized asset with increased and reliable income, significantly raising its value in the process.

Making improvements to the property will not only serve to attract new tenants, but also keep the existing tenants in place. Extending the leases of existing tenants is another way to add value to the property through leasing. In the spirit of giving to get, I often negotiate an extended lease from a tenant in exchange for improving some aspect of their unit, such as installing new carpet or a new AC unit. By extending a tenant's lease, you fatten up the property's projected NOI, making your property that much more attractive to prospective buyers.

Value Add #3: Reduce Operating Expenses

By leasing up, you significantly increase your property's gross income. In order to maximize your property's net income, you will need to take a good hard look at the property's operating expenses, and identify where they can be reduced. When buying underperforming assets I specifically target mismanaged properties, which I identify by comparing the expense reports for that property with other comparable properties in the area. More often than not, I find wasteful spending in areas that the previous owner never would have thought to look, simply because he/she had always done things in a certain way.

When looking for ways to reduce expenses, keep in mind that the bulk of a property's expenses are fixed, meaning they are the same whether you have an empty building or a full one. The only expenses that really fluctuate with occupancy are utilities and janitorial costs, which are minimal in the scheme of things. Payroll for property management, insurance, and property tax are all fixed expenses, and account for the bulk of a property's operational costs.

One of the biggest ways to cut costs is to reduce payroll expenses by keeping property management in-house, as opposed to hiring a third-party management company. Having your own property manager onsite will be not only less expensive, but a more efficient and effective way of meeting your tenants' ongoing needs as well.

Another thing to consider as you grow your portfolio is that if you end up acquiring multiple properties in the same area, you can easily consolidate the management of these properties.

Case in point: I bought four buildings within blocks of each other, and appointed one property manager with a golf cart to manage all four. We also consolidated the day porters and the building engineers. For the four buildings I just mentioned, I cut the payroll by half when I took over. I now have one chief engineer, two assistant engineers, one property manager and one administrator, saving a total of about $150,000 per year.

Other costs that can often be reduced through consolidation are the maintenance expenses. In order to get a better rate on property maintenance costs such as roofing, plumbing, and electrical repairs, I try to deal exclusively with one company. Developing a strong relationship with your vendors, and consolidating their services as much as possible, will go a long way towards reducing your property's overall expenses.

Insurance is yet another cost that can often be reduced, simply by taking the time to gather quotes from a number of insurance agents. When choosing a policy, take great care not to underinsure the property. If you have your auto, home, and business insurance with multiple companies, try to consolidate with one company—this will almost always reduce your overall premiums. Find out if there's anything you can do to reduce the premiums further, such as adding an alarm, or putting in a leak detection system. Last but not least, bid the insurance out every year to ensure you are getting the best rate possible—if nothing else, it will keep your provider on its toes!

In certain states, you can also reduce expenses by hiring a law firm to file property tax appeals for your properties. In Texas, for example, the property assessment laws are complicated, with properties being reappraised annually by the county and city. In other states, like California, you don't need a law firm to appeal your property taxes, because properties are not reassessed at more than a 2 percent increase per year.

The need to hire a law firm will vary depending on the property tax structure of the state in which you live. Some states reassess the property taxes every year, and some reassess them only when they are sold. Knowing the property tax structure in your state and taking appropriate action to reduce these costs can cut your property's annual expenses dramatically. For more information on how property assessment works in your area, look up your county assessor's office online.

Final Thoughts

By now, you are starting to see the Big Picture of making your money on the buy. In the first stage, you use the under-performing aspects of a property to secure a highly discounted price; in the next, you use them as the basis upon which to add value, so you can maximize your ROI when it's time to sell.

Just think, many investors never learn the thrill of discovering a diamond in the rough. It's one thing to buy a beautiful property, and another to buy the ugly duckling and, as a direct result of your efforts, watch it turn into a swan. That is true pride of ownership. It's one of my favorite things about playing this amazing game, and one of the greatest benefits of investing the contrarian way.

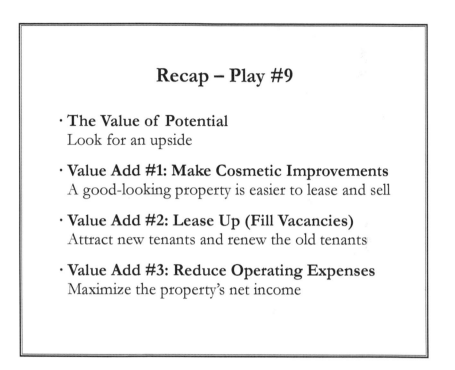

Recap – Play #9

· **The Value of Potential**
  Look for an upside

· **Value Add #1: Make Cosmetic Improvements**
  A good-looking property is easier to lease and sell

· **Value Add #2: Lease Up (Fill Vacancies)**
  Attract new tenants and renew the old tenants

· **Value Add #3: Reduce Operating Expenses**
  Maximize the property's net income

Play #10

Actively Manage
Your Properties

Take a Hands-On Approach
to Property Management

One of the things I learned early on in my real estate career is that in order to build a truly successful real estate portfolio, it is essential to be personally involved with the management of your properties. Among other things, being hands-on with your property management by keeping it in-house will both reduce your operating expenses and ensure that you always know what is going on with your properties.

I used to hire third-party companies for all of my property management, until I noticed that it was neither very efficient nor very cost-effective to outsource it. By bringing it in-house, I ended up saving between $50,000 and $60,000 per month in management fees. (Note: If you only own one building in an area, it may not be practical or cost effective to do this.)

What's more, being hands-on with the management of your properties will result in much happier tenants, and happy tenants are an essential part of keeping your properties performing with a steady income level.

Maintain a Consistent Onsite Presence

More than anything, tenants love responsiveness. It is not an exaggeration to say that having an onsite manager will often make the difference between your tenants staying or leaving when their leases expire. (It should go without saying that this does not apply to the management of an SFR or a condo.) Take a moment to think about it from the perspective of the tenant: With onsite management, they can walk down the hall to the leasing office and talk to someone anytime they have a question or a concern, vs. having to call a remote offsite management office, where they may get an answering machine and have to wait to have their needs addressed. With onsite management you are more likely to keep your tenants, because you will be providing them with a much higher level of service. Also, when you can say you have onsite management in your advertising, you will fill your vacancies a lot faster.

Treat Your Tenants Like Your Partners

As a landlord, the worst thing you can do is nickel and dime your tenants. That is a surefire way to make them unhappy, which will make them more inclined to move on when their leases come up for renewal. Find another way to improve your bottom line: You could focus on cutting costs, or filling vacancies.

If you think about it, your tenants are your partners, and they will help you get to your $100 million portfolio. The landlord-tenant relationship is very, very key. Whether you are holding or selling, having happy tenants is a value. Happy tenants who are planning on renewing their leases will boost your current and projected NOI, which will help you sell at a higher price.

Knowing how important the landlord-tenant relationship is, start going the extra mile for your tenants the moment you take ownership. When I first purchase a property, my property management staff immediately sends out an introduction letter and survey to all of the tenants in order to find out what they like and don't like about the property. Some of the tenants might be fed up already with something the previous owner didn't fix, no matter how many times it was brought up as a concern. In order to give these tenants the message that you are not that kind of landlord, you need to roll up your sleeves, identify their concerns, and address them right off the bat.

Another way to keep your tenants happy is to have the onsite management check in with them on a monthly or twice-monthly basis, preferably in person, to make sure that all of their needs are being met. Most tenants are accustomed to never being contacted by the landlord unless they are late paying rent. Going out of your way to establish and maintain communication with your tenants will give you a very competitive edge as a landlord—and considering you will most likely be holding during an economic down cycle, which is typically a tenant's market, a competitive edge is a very good thing to have.

To that effect I always go out of my way to reach out to my tenants on the holidays; each year we send out chocolates and cards, and hire a Christmas tree service to set up a tree in the lobby. You would be surprised how much of a difference something as simple as a box of chocolates can make! Go the extra mile to please your tenants, and it will pay off for you in many ways.

Give to Get with Your Tenants

Your Contrarian PlayBook negotiation skills will serve you as a landlord, just as they serve you when you are buying and selling. Negotiation with your tenants usually revolves around the renewal of their lease agreements. In the interest of keeping your tenants, be prepared to give to get during this negotiation process.

If a tenant is leaning towards leaving, find out why. If they have specific concerns, find out what they are, and address them if you can. If their concerns are financial, offer them a slightly reduced lease rate, on the condition that they extend the lease by an additional one or two years. If their concerns are more material, you can use this same approach: Offer to buy them a new AC unit or replace their carpet, as the case may be, in exchange for a longer lease term. This way, both parties win. In all likelihood, the tenant would rather not go through the upheaval of moving to a new location—and you certainly don't want to have to standardize and lease out another vacancy, if it can be avoided. Give to get. At the end of the day, the more time left on the tenants' leases when you sell, the higher your sale price will be, and the closer you will be to your $100 million portfolio.

Final Thoughts

The Contrarian PlayBook strategy is not about holding your properties for a long time. In fact, I sell most of my properties within two to four years. Some might assume that this means that property management is not an important component of my strategy. To the contrary, it is essential! The better the property management, the more valuable the property, and the more money made.

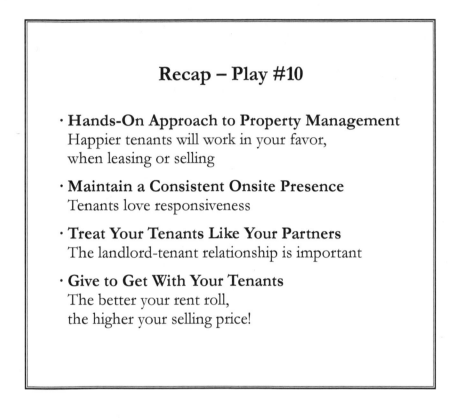

Recap – Play #10

· **Hands-On Approach to Property Management**
Happier tenants will work in your favor,
when leasing or selling

· **Maintain a Consistent Onsite Presence**
Tenants love responsiveness

· **Treat Your Tenants Like Your Partners**
The landlord-tenant relationship is important

· **Give to Get With Your Tenants**
The better your rent roll,
the higher your selling price!

Play #11

Actively Manage Your Portfolio

Portfolio Management is Key

Portfolio (asset) management is at the core of the Contrarian PlayBook. In order to build your portfolio to that $100 million mark, you will need to master the art of portfolio management, which is found in the balance of selling and holding your current properties while continuing to accumulate new properties. If you can achieve this balance, you will be light-years ahead of the pack!

Ten years ago my portfolio consisted of two homes, a shopping center in Santa Ana, and a second shopping center in Whittier. Had I not sold these properties and used the liquidity to buy bigger and more valuable assets, today I would be worth $2 million, $3 million at the most. Today, as you know, my portfolio value exceeds $100 million. At the time that I sold those four original properties, I had friends—some of them fellow real estate investors—telling me that I was crazy to unload such stable, profitable assets, especially since I had bought them with good, secure loans at favorable rates. They couldn't see what I could see, which was that those properties were worth infinitely more to me as moving pieces than they were just sitting in my portfolio. I didn't want to get comfortable at that level of success— I was determined not to lose sight of my long-term goals. I knew that I had to make my money work for me, and the only way to do that was to use those properties to buy and leverage my way up into more strategically valuable assets.

Be An Active Investor

Being an active investor is an important part of successful portfolio management. Active investors are always seeking ways to grow their portfolios—to put it simply, an active investor never grows complacent.

Complacency ranks right up there with fear and greed as a major threat to the growth of your portfolio, and therefore the growth of your wealth. Many investors reach a point in their careers where they stop seeing new possibilities, even stop looking for them, because they get comfortable with where they are, and attached to the properties they own. They settle into the steady income that their properties provide. Their drive to achieve their long-term goals by growing their portfolios is gradually displaced by an attachment to what wealth they have built, and eventually they no longer see what they can create—only what they are afraid to lose!

As an active investor, I buy and sell properties fast. As you know, I keep my properties for an average of two to four years, which is not at all long in the real estate world. Of course there will be times when you have to hold a property for a few years until the market comes back up, but as an active investor, you must always remember that your properties are meant to be kept in motion, not to sit in your portfolio collecting dust. Only by selling or effectively leveraging your properties will you be able to grow your portfolio to the tune of $100 million.

Liquidity is Essential

Active investors know that liquidity is a prime factor in growing their portfolios, because liquidity is what will allow you to leverage the properties you own into more properties and more profits. The more money you have to buy with, the more money you can make on your buys!

The two major sources of liquidity are your cash reserves and your properties, as described below.

Cash Reserves

The worst thing you can do as a real estate investor in any market cycle is to run out of money. Since every market cycle is going to offer you a unique set of opportunities to increase the value of your portfolio, in one way or another, you will want to have cash reserves at all times—so never invest all of your money.

Your cash reserves are also your number one source of liquidity. Money is a power tool, and you will be able to achieve your long-term goals much faster by keeping some on hand.

Let Your Properties Work for You

There are two ways in which your properties can provide liquidity: You can sell or refinance them. I personally prefer to sell a property rather than refinance, because when you sell you get your equity for free (in other words, no interest), but when you borrow the equity you are paying interest on the loan. In the end, whether you sell or refinance depends largely on the market.

If the timing is not right to sell, and you need to create some liquidity in order to add to your portfolio, refinancing your existing properties is a great option to have. Refinancing can be difficult during a recession because the banks will usually have a lot of under-performing assets on their books, but if this is your best option you have nothing to lose by talking to your banker(s). If your property is profitable, and you can demonstrate that you have added significant value to it through the improvements you have made, lenders may just work with you.

For most beginning investors, liquidity issues can be a problem, but no matter what, don't sell off property at a loss. If you are unable to secure financing at reasonable terms, sit tight. If you followed the criteria we covered in Plays #5 and #7, your properties will be paying for themselves, so you should be able to weather recessions regardless of your refI options, or lack thereof.

Timing is Everything

As a contrarian you see the big picture of real estate, and therefore you know that if you are actively managing your portfolio by buying, selling and holding properties, every point on the real estate cycle offers opportunities.

When the market is up, you can sell at a profit. When the market is down, you can hold the properties you have, add value to them, and lease them for income. The troughs in the real estate cycles also present opportunities to acquire more properties for your portfolio. In fact, many of the properties I sell at peak I end up buying back at steep discounts when the market goes down again!

Since we discussed buying in such detail in the previous plays, we will assume that you have a very firm sense of when to buy, and how to pick winning properties. Deciding when to sell or hold is our focus in this play. Do note that many of the same resources you use to determine the timing of your buys will be used again for your sell vs. hold decisions.

Sell High – Just Do It!

You know that fear and greed can be the biggest stumbling blocks when buying properties. You know the importance of keeping your emotions out of the equation, keeping your eye on the prize, and being willing to give in order to get. All of this is equally true, and just as important, when it comes to selling your properties.

Sell Like a Contrarian

The contrarian is all about being on the right side of the cycle. My instinct for getting out (selling) at the right time has been a critical part of my success. I am willing to get out before the price peaks–in other words, I don't get greedy and try to hold on for the absolute top of the market cycle. The investors who do that often find themselves on the wrong side of the curve. The contrarian sees profit on the table and takes it, and keeps investing. Look at the numbers. If you're happy with the money you're making, pull that trigger and make the sale, then move on to the next deal!

Selling for the Liquidity

Since my investment strategy is about increasing the value of my portfolio, I always keep my eye on the bigger picture. Having the resources to buy other properties may be more fruitful than worrying about a little more profit on a particular sale. In the end, your profits from being an active investor will be larger than the bit more money you might have made waiting for a peak price. Don't be afraid to sell for liquidity–it is a key component of the Contrarian PlayBook strategy.

In 2004, I bought three buildings for $9.6 million. I sold them for $13.75 million in 2005 when I saw that the property cap rates in that market were becoming unreasonable. Four years later, I bought those same three buildings back for $5.7 million–this time as foreclosures from the bank! This is a great example of the payoff of active investing!

Timing the Market: Test the Waters

As I mentioned before, timing the market is not an exact science–in fact, it is more of an art. Pinpointing the very peak of a seller's market is impossible, so sometimes the best way to know if it's the right time to sell is to test the waters by putting your property on the market.

As an example, let's say you have a 4-unit residential income property, which you bought a year and a half ago in a recession at 75 percent occupancy. In that time you have added value by leasing it up and making cosmetic improvements. The improvements you've made have allowed you to bump each unit's rent by $100 per month, increasing the property's annual rental revenues by $4,800, which has added even further to the property's value.

When you see the market coming up, test the waters by putting the property on the market. As a rule of thumb, I will price the property at 5 percent over the last comparable sale. If you're getting low offers or no offers, it's time to hold—but remember, you're in a great position to hold and hold comfortably, because you've made your money on the buy, increased your property's value, and are getting income from the property. On the other hand, if people start bidding against each other in a buying frenzy, and you're being offered more than your asking price, it's definitely time to sell.

Give to Get – Again

Once you receive an offer and go into escrow, be willing to make some concessions to your buyer in order to close the deal. Being open to making concessions as a seller is every bit as important as making concessions as a buyer—remember, the ultimate goal is to get the deal done so you can move on to bigger and better things!

As a seller, you will probably encounter a glitch in every deal you make. One of the most common scenarios you will encounter is having your buyer discover during the tenant interview portion of due diligence that a major tenant is leaving in two years. If they want to back out as a result, offer them a year (or even two) of that tenant's rent in the form of a price reduction. You will be able to write that off as a loss on your taxes, so you will make some of it back in the short term—and the rest you will make back many times over by reinvesting your earnings in other income properties! Never walk away from profit, and don't let your ego interfere with making concessions to get the deal done—don't step over a dollar to get to a penny!

A word about offering seller financing: I very rarely offer seller financing to prospective buyers, because with the rate of growth I expect from my portfolio, the interest I would earn from seller financing simply does not cut it. This being said, seller financing is appealing to those who would like the fixed income without the responsibility of property management. Ultimately, you will need to decide whether or not offering seller financing is compatible with your long-term goal.

Never Say Never

Buying low and selling high is as close to an absolute truth as you can get in real estate—but even this most sensible of rules can get in the way of seeing new opportunities if you take it to extremes. Most of my wealth has been created by buying in down cycles and selling in up cycles, because that is how you make your money on the buy—but never say never!

Recessions offer unbelievably great buying opportunities—if you have the liquidity, the right team, the strategic wherewithal, and the contrarian mindset to capitalize on them. From June to August of 2008, I bought twenty-four REO homes, all from banks. I never would have foreseen myself investing so heavily in residential real estate—least of all SFRs—but when I saw that the recession had created the buying opportunity of a lifetime, I couldn't resist! After some minor remodeling I rented them all out, which provided me with steady cash flow right off the bat.

Now the twist on the formula: By early 2011 I had sold twelve at a profit, representing a very rare exception to the rule of not selling in a recession. I sold these homes during a brief, mid-recession surge in SFR sales that came as a result of President Obama's $8,000 tax incentive for home buyers. For three short months there was a big spike in the single-family dwelling market, and it was in this window of time that I saw the opportunity to sell some of the houses at a profit and increase my liquidity in the process.

Under ordinary circumstances I would never advise anyone to sell in a recession, but this story is a perfect example of the fact that there is an exception to even the most logical of rules. As an active investor, I saw the window of opportunity, did some dollar cost averaging, and decided that even though I would make more money on those homes by waiting for the opportunity to sell higher, I would make more still by liquidating those assets at a smaller profit and reinvesting the capital into more lucrative commercial income properties. While the circumstances of those sales were extremely specific to that time and place, I share this story with you because it so clearly illustrates the importance of being an active investor, keeping up on even minor fluctuations in the economy, and having the big picture in mind as you manage your portfolio.

When all is said and done, my system does not specifically revolve around buying in a recession, or buying foreclosures, or buying distressed assets, or flipping houses; it revolves around buying discounted properties, and selling them at a profit. There are deals to be found in any market, and while the vast majority of the time you will be best off buying during a recession and selling into an economic boom, there are exceptions, however rare, to every rule. Always keep your eyes open for opportunity in unexpected places.

Know How to Hold

The three main stages of portfolio management are buying, holding, and selling. Knowing when to hold is simple–you hold when it's not time to sell! Holding is simply the by-product of not selling. To a certain extent, you're going to be forced to hold during down cycles, but this is far from wasted time.

Hold Like an Active Investor

Knowing when to hold is simple; knowing how to hold is more involved. As the active investor knows, "holding" does not mean sitting on your hands and waiting for the next seller's market to present itself. The holding period in portfolio management is a very active one, and becomes increasingly so as your wealth grows. Eventually, you will be utilizing this time to expand your portfolio by acquiring more discounted assets at incredible prices. When you're holding, you're getting income, a tax write-off on depreciation of the improvements, and potential to cash out by refinancing. It is also a good time to add value to your properties by fixing them up, leasing them out, and streamlining operational costs.

With all of the emphasis on buying and selling, don't underestimate the importance of the holding stage of investment. Remember, how you handle your properties while you own them is a large part of how you increase their value in order to sell at a profit, and therefore critical to your success in real estate.

Final Thoughts

As you travel the path to your own $100 million portfolio, don't lose sight of the fact that every one of your properties needs to be an active part of your continued success. Remember that your properties are tools to help you achieve your long-term goals–they are not meant to sit around. Make them work for you whether you are buying, selling, or holding, in each and every cycle of the market! Keep your eyes open for new opportunities, never grow complacent, and enjoy the game.

Recap – Play #11

- **Portfolio Management is Key**
  Balance buying with leasing and selling

  - **Be an Active Investor**
    Sell and leverage your way to your
    $100 million real estate portfolio

  - **Liquidity is Essential**
    - **Cash Reserves**
    - **Let Your Properties Work for You**

  - **Timing is Everything**
    When the market is up, sell at a profit
    When the market is down, buy at a discount

- **Sell High–Just Do It!**
  - **Sell Like a Contrarian**
    Keep your eye on the bigger picture

  - **Selling for the Liquidity**
    Make your properties work for you

  - **Timing the Market–
    Test the Waters**
    Put your property on the market
    and see what happens

  - **Give to Get–Again**
    Get the deal done

  - **Never Say Never**
    Deals can be found in any market

- **Know How to Hold**
  Hold when it is not time to sell

  - **Hold Like an Active Investor**
    Don't sit on your hands

Play #12

Expand Your Horizons

Expand Your Portfolio

Now that you know the basics of the Contrarian PlayBook strategy, I want to give you a look at what could happen when you decide you are ready to expand your horizons by investing outside of your local area.

Opening up your investing beyond the boundaries of your local market is a big step, but will allow you to continually grow your portfolio. If at a given time you aren't finding good investment options in your area, opportunity may be knocking somewhere else! New territories will offer up a whole new range of investment possibilities, and will enable you to grow your portfolio much more quickly. On this I speak from personal experience—as you will read below, I never would have been able to grow my portfolio so quickly if I hadn't begun investing in other states.

At this point in the playbook, I hope that you have taken the contrarian mindset to heart and know the exhilaration of staying ahead of the curve—because it is now time to take this show on the road!

50 Economies

Real estate markets vary, and in the United States—where each state has its own economy, demographics, and sectors of business—it is almost as if there are 50 different countries. That said, all of these economies share the same great federal tax benefits for real estate investors. This means that if the real estate market in one state is too high, you can find another state that offers more discounted properties.

As always, your goal is to buy in the down cycle and sell in an up cycle, and when you think on a national scale, there will be plenty of opportunities for this. In the early 2000's, I switched from California to Arizona to Texas to North Carolina, back to California, and then back to Texas again! Because of this strategy, I continuously increased the value of my portfolio despite the recession.

Note that when I expanded to other states, I focused my investing exclusively on commercial properties. Residential can be very management intensive, so if you are buying and leasing in another state, shifting your focus to commercial properties makes good common sense.

Put a Team Together

When you begin buying in a new state you will also want to be thinking in terms of creating a team there. A good starting point would be to find some real estate agents who know the local area. You can gather a pile of statistical and demographic data, but it will often pale in comparison to the information you can get from a local real estate professional.

With this in mind, when you come across a property that fits your criteria, use the initial phone call to the agent to introduce yourself as a serious investor, not just for that specific property, but in general. Be open to how you can create a mutually beneficial relationship with each real estate professional you talk to. When you talk to them, ask them for recommendations for the other local team members you will be seeking: Brokers, property managers, contractors, real estate and tax attorneys, to name a few. This will help you to quickly build a strong team in your new territory.

The Contrarian PlayBook– In Action!

The best way for me to show you how lucrative it can be to expand your investing is to share my own experiences. When I took the leap and began investing outside of California, my opportunities–and my wealth–multiplied exponentially. My hope is that it will inspire you, when the time is right, to do the same. Let's Gooooo!

Time to Expand

By late 2003, the California real estate market was hot, hot, hot–and it was making me nervous. Prices were going up monthly and people were buying any real estate they could find. The real estate values had become purely speculative because of the market frenzy. I knew that because of the high prices and 1031 exchange requirements, investors would soon start looking elsewhere in order to avoid paying taxes on their capital gains.

At that point I had bought and sold over 30 properties, mostly in the Long Beach, California area. The rental rates were capping out, and I realized it was time to get out of California.

Arizona

Since I lived in California and had until then only invested in local property, I began looking at office buildings in the neighboring states of Arizona, Nevada, and Oregon. I found that high-flying speculation had created a bubble in Nevada, and so I didn't want to go there. In Oregon there were not enough listings or activity. In Arizona, which was in a downcycle, I found many properties priced at a low dollar per square foot, with the right cap rates and multiple price reductions, which meant that there was value to be found there.

In making this move to Arizona, I decided against investing in apartment buildings or any other residential properties. My experience had taught me that these types of property were very management intensive, and I knew that being in another state would make hands-on management impossible at first.

At the time I was looking for a multi-tenant commercial office building with at least a 9 percent return. In keeping with the criteria, it also needed to be priced at a significant discount to its replacement cost and located on a major street.

I found several properties that fit the bill, but one in particular stood out. The price had been reduced twice and it had been on the market for many months. I called the agent and found out that there were three owners who had had a dispute, and two of them wanted out. Here was a great window of opportunity.

I decided it was time to go to Arizona to see the property and meet with the sellers. The sellers had purchased the property five years back at a price of $1.8 million. The property was 50,000 square feet in a one-story multi-tenant office park and was 75 percent occupied at the time. They had started by asking $1.8 million but reduced it to $1.5 million.

At this point in my real estate investment career, I had the power and leverage of cash, so I offered them $1.2 million with a 20-day escrow. They refused and said they would make a counter offer. The next day they countered at $1.4 million. In the end, I negotiated a final deal at $1.325 million ($30 per square foot) and got a 2 percent referral fee since I represented myself in the transaction.

I cleaned up the property, reduced its expenses, and increased the occupancy. The Arizona market, as I had predicted, started to pick up, and after ten months I sold the property for $1.85 million to a California investor.

My next move, after several months of research, was to buy two four-story multi-tenant medical office buildings. These buildings appealed to me partly because I had learned that medical tenants, as compared to most office building tenants, were less likely to move out due to the extensive improvements and equipment installation required for their offices. I purchased both buildings for approximately $8 million. In this case, I chose to finance the properties because they had high cap rates, which provided easy financing. When the cost of borrowing is much lower than your cap rate, than financing is your best option—why not make money with the bank's money?

By mid 2004 I had purchased $10 million worth of office property in Phoenix, Arizona, and found that I had been spot on in predicting that California investors would be looking for out-of-state buying opportunities to satisfy their 1031 exchange requirements. Good contrarian that I am, I had gone to Arizona well ahead of the curve, and so I had properties to sell them—at a significant profit! I was now a multi-millionaire. Arizona had been very good to me.

Texas

At this point, the Arizona market was sizzling hot, and you know how that makes me nervous. Anytime you have investors buying with their eyes closed, you have to question the sustainability of the market. I knew that the real estate price increase had a cap; I also knew that once property values began to exceed replacement costs, the builders would start a building frenzy. That would mean more vacancies, due to the saturation of supply. Because of these factors, I was reluctant to reinvest my cash proceeds into Arizona properties, so in 2004 I turned to Texas.

Why Texas? As I mentioned in Play #2, the research I was doing online indicated that due to the bust of the oil companies, Texas had still not fully recovered from its early 1980s real estate depression. The economy in Texas is now more diversified, but at the time it was heavily concentrated in petroleum, so when oil prices crashed it sent the whole state's economy into a tailspin. I realized that the price of oil was rising (over $40 per barrel at the time), and so I predicted that the economy in Texas would soon head up.

Best of all, Texas real estate was priced substantially lower than replacement costs, and properties were selling at a very high return compared to California or Arizona. I also realized that once investors sold in Arizona, Florida, California, and Nevada, they would again be looking for a place to reinvest their money.

After investigating several Texan cities, including Midland, Dallas, Houston, and Corpus Christi, I used Loopnet to find a ten-story building in Midland that was priced at $50 per square foot. I purchased a ticket and flew to Midland to tour the property and the area. As I landed in the very small airport, I noticed many empty buildings and a lot of raw land. I did not get a good vibe. Within a few hours, I was touring the building with the agent. The building was a single tenant building leasing to an oil and gas-related company, with only five years remaining on the lease. I decided not to purchase the property for three reasons: 1) The single tenant posed a significant risk, 2) the area was depressed with lots of empty buildings, and 3) the submarket was not a large one.

I then flew to Corpus ChristI and looked at several properties, which I decided to pass on as well, mainly due to the lack of inventory and sales activity, which indicated too small of a submarket. Exit strategy is always an important factor to consider, so you need to be sure that the market is liquid enough to be able to sell down the line.

This left Dallas and Houston, and I chose Houston, because it is a major metropolitan city and had the most listings. I flew in and found five buildings that were being marketed by the same seller. They were 3-5 story office buildings in the suburbs of Houston with an average occupancy of 83 percent at $54 per square foot (significantly below replacement cost), and they were all multi-tenant buildings with positive cash flow. Clearly, these buildings did not fit the occupancy criteria listed in Play

#5, but in this case the properties presented with a good cap rate, and were listed at a reduced price, so I went for it.

I cherry picked three of them and negotiated a deal of $9.6 million with a $2.5 million down payment—and I managed to get a $200,000 referral fee since I represented myself in the deal! The seller was motivated because he had formed a partnership five years earlier when the Texas market was on an upswing, and his partners were pushing to sell and close the fund. I knew I was getting a bargain.

I concentrated on leasing up the vacant spaces and reduced some of the operation costs. I ended up selling the properties for $13.7 million, netting $3.8 million in profits. My predictions about Texas had come true—oil prices kept rising (above $50 per barrel) and 1031 money was flowing in. I now had many investors wanting me to pick properties and buy for them, so I had to hire more staff, including a full-time attorney to write all the contracts and leases.

By 2005, my portfolio had grown to include 1.5 million square feet of real estate! I was paying almost $1 million in annual management fees to a third party brokerage firm to manage my Texas properties, so I formed The Khoshbin Company, Inc. as a management company and took it all in-house. I also formed my first Khoshbin Fund (Private Placement) and purchased an office building in Amarillo, Texas, which we sold for a 30 percent profit a year later.

Between 2004 and 2007, I had completed over $400 million in real estate transactions and had over 2.2 million square feet under management, of which 1.2 million square feet I owned personally—but I didn't stop there!

In 2008, just like Arizona, the Houston market hit its cap. No economy expands or recesses forever—what goes up must come down. Knowing that the market usually fluctuates in 2-3 year cycles, I had a feeling that Houston had capped out, and was going to be coming down. Because multi-tenant office properties are particularly vulnerable to recessions, I decided it was the right time to sell off some of my office buildings.

I shifted my focus to industrial buildings, in part because I knew that industrial tenants require minimal tenant improvements. (Note: This is true in the context of my strategy, because if you are following it, you will not be buying new construction. One of the downsides to industrial real estate is that if you are buying new, tenant improvements are typically very costly.) Without the cost of tenant improvements, the operating expenses for the industrial property landlord are very low.

Not only are TI minimal with industrial properties, but industrial tenants, as you know, are far more vested in their leaseholds than office tenants. For this reason, industrial properties are less susceptible to tenant loss in a tenant's market. With these factors in mind I knew that it was the right time for me to shift my focus from office properties to industrial assets, even though they offer a lower ROI.

North Carolina, Ohio, and Pennsylvania

When I shifted my Texas holdings from high rise office buildings to industrial properties, I also bought four retail shopping centers in North Carolina, Ohio, and Pennsylvania. Remember, as with industrial tenants, retail tenants are also more vested in their leaseholds than office tenants, and therefore far less likely to move in a tenant's market. In selecting these properties, I was again looking for attractive cap rates and significantly reduced prices. The retail shopping centers I bought in North Carolina caught my eye because they had solid anchors in the form of very profitable grocery stores, so it was a safe bet. By that time, I was looking to park my money in low-risk assets because I was sensing an upcoming storm—the Great Recession.

I found all of these properties on Loopnet, and visited each of them before making the decision to add them to my portfolio. Even though I didn't have any broker connections in any of these places, I was able to gather more information about the local economies and the properties' histories from the listing brokers.

Back to California

I had always planned to invest in California properties again. When I sold all of my investments in California in 2003, I also knew that I would return to the market when I could buy foreclosures. In 2008, as I predicted, real estate in California, Florida, and Nevada (all states that had been the subject of a buying frenzy and had overbuilt) started to make a significant downturn, so I looked to buy. Again, as a contrarian player who stays ahead of the curve, I re-entered the California market as others were leaving.

As I mentioned in Play #11, after years of focusing exclusively on commercial real estate, I found myself looking at the residential market in California again. After researching online, I focused my search on Orange County. I used an MLS site to search which cities in Orange County had the most REO listings, and found that Santa Ana did.

In addition to having the highest population of any city in the county, my research also revealed that it was the fourth most densely populated city in the U.S., and I knew this translated to the highest demand for housing in Orange County. Because of these factors, I realized it would be a great place to own rental properties. Within 60 days I purchased 24 foreclosed homes from the banks. After minor remodeling, I quickly rented them out, establishing a profitable cash flow. My investors wanted in, and together we purchased 90 homes in the next 6 months!

Knowing that residential management requires a high degree of attention, and believing in hands-on management whenever possible, I created a residential management department in my company.

In early 2009, the California housing market experienced a brief upturn, and investors and first-time homebuyers began to buy–so I began to sell! The curve in the road was approaching, and I knew it was time to move again.

Back to Texas

Not one to burn bridges, I realized that office buildings in Houston were again a good buy. Five out of the nine high-rises that I had sold two to three years earlier were in foreclosure. Others were selling for 50-60 percent below the price I sold them for.

I found a six-story office building that was a distressed sale. I was able to purchase the property for $35 per square foot. The property was 55 percent occupied and still cash flow positive. I had previously owned the two 12-story high-rise office build-ings adjacent to this property, so I was familiar with the submar-ket. Having sold those two towers for approximately $70 per square foot, I knew that $35 per square foot for this property was an incredible bargain.

To this day, I own six mid-rise office buildings in Houston, one of which I had previously sold for $70 per square foot, and was able to buy back for $16 per square foot!

Beyond State Lines

You can see how I have used the contrarian game plan to expand my portfolio, beyond state lines and beyond $100 million! Opening up my investing to other states changed my game completely, and allowed me to build my portfolio with a speed that would not have been possible had I never looked beyond California.

While expanding your portfolio in this way is a major step, it is an important one to take if you want to make the most of the Contrarian PlayBook strategy. That said, investing in other states is something I only recommend to experienced investors.

When to Expand to New Territories

Knowing when to expand to new territories is a key element of being an active investor, and staying ahead of the curve. When you begin to invest in other states, you will continue to use everything you have learned in this playbook. The same strategy applies, but you are enlarging your vision to include all 50 states, or in other words, all 50 economies.

As always, do your homework. The same sources that you use to find both demographic and statistical information, as well as available properties, for your local area or state, can often be used for other cities and states. Just as I made my first out-of-state investments in states that I could easily travel to from California, I recommend that you make your first out-of-state buys in states relatively close to where you live. This will simplify your life as you are learning the ins and outs of investing in new territories. When doing your research you will want to review the opportunities in several states, eventually narrowing it down to specific submarkets in your chosen state.

As to when you are ready for this step, only you can determine this. Take an honest look at your risk tolerance, and understand that buying outside of your local area can have its challenges. That said, if you have truly absorbed the strategy of the Contrarian PlayBook, and you have a solid foundation of experience, challenges are no problem! While you do not have to go out-of-state to grow your portfolio, doing so will multiply your opportunities, and put you on the fast track to your $100 million portfolio.

Final Thoughts

This is the closing play in the Contrarian PlayBook, but I hope that this book is the opening shot for your own very successful real estate investment ventures. Together we have traveled from goal setting to your $100 million real estate portfolio, from gathering your team to investing nationwide, from making a first buy to managing a whole portfolio. Wow!

In this book, I wanted to expand your vision about real estate investment. In this play, I wanted to expand your vision of where you can go as a real estate investor–which is to say, wherever you want! That is the great thing about this game plan: You can take it on the road, and–if I do say so myself– it travels very, very well.

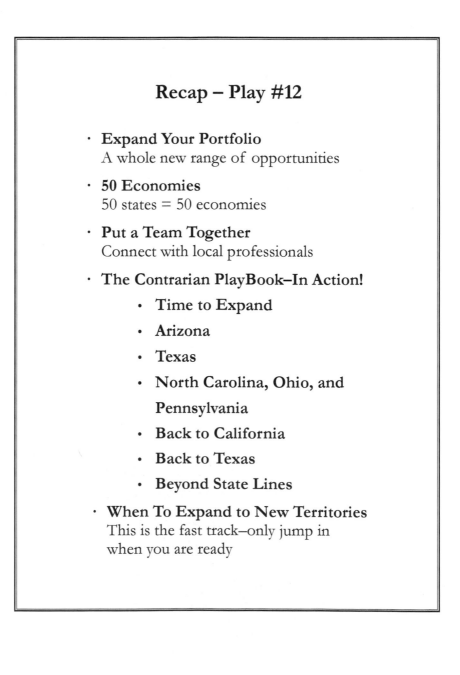

Recap – Play #12

- **Expand Your Portfolio**
  A whole new range of opportunities

- **50 Economies**
  50 states = 50 economies

- **Put a Team Together**
  Connect with local professionals

- **The Contrarian PlayBook–In Action!**
  - **Time to Expand**
  - **Arizona**
  - **Texas**
  - **North Carolina, Ohio, and Pennsylvania**
  - **Back to California**
  - **Back to Texas**
  - **Beyond State Lines**

- **When To Expand to New Territories**
  This is the fast track–only jump in when you are ready

Afterword
From One Contrarian to Another

Following the Contrarian PlayBook strategy requires common sense, independent thought, and above all, cojones! Fortunately, as a contrarian investor, you have all of these things in spades. So don't sit on your couch waiting for the weatherman to give you the forecast—just look out the window! Step outside of the box and use your common sense. What the weathermen out there don't want you to know is that these days, common sense and the internet can get you just about anywhere. All the information you need to make your next move is right at your fingertips.

On a personal note, I will say that investing in real estate is as much fun as I have ever had. I truly hope that after reading my Contrarian PlayBook, you are as excited as I am about all the possibilities that real estate investment can bring. I have given you a great game plan that shows you how to power up, make your money on the buy, and stay in the game—and the benefit of any good game plan is that it gives you a solid foundation, from which you can truly soar. So join me on this path to financial freedom and turn your desires into action, your dreams into reality, and your real estate portfolio into $100 million.

Let's Gooooo!

INDEX

About the Author

Manny Khoshbin is President and CEO of The Khoshbin Company, based in Orange County, California. His company has real estate holdings in seven states, totaling over 2.5 million square feet. Khoshbin immigrated to the United States with his family in 1984, at the age of 14. He got his real estate license in 1992, and proceeded to build a tremendously successful career in real estate. Khoshbin lives in Newport Coast, California, with his wife Leyla and their two dogs, Lupe and Coco.

About The Khoshbin Company

Founded by Manny Khoshbin, The Khoshbin Company is a commercial real estate management and investment company based in Irvine, California. With a proven track record of highly profitable investing in distressed property markets, The Khoshbin Company's strong combination of management skills, leasing strategy, and insightful market experience has set it apart in the industry. For more information, visit:

www.thekhoshbincompany.com

Made in the USA
Lexington, KY
23 February 2015